Four Seasons of Trou

Four Seasons of Trout

A Fly-fisher's Year

John Parsons

Drawings by Angela Müller

HarperCollinsPublishers New Zealand

The following chapters have been published previously as articles in the periodicals named:

In *New Zealand Fisherman*:
Trio of Hobbses
Cover up!
Bob Bragg, angler
Statistics are important

In *Rod & Rifle*:
Unabridged:
Spring's here!
Skues would have been disgusted
Where they came from
Hedgehoggers revealed
Farewell, Killer Bug
Biter bit
Two from The Point
Hysteria at Whakaipo

Abridged:
A mayflies man
Good luck, Fred!
Tribute to Greg
It's De Lautour at last!
Our first book of trout-fishing

First published 1994
HarperCollins*Publishers (New Zealand) Limited*
P.O. Box 1, Auckland

Copyright © John Parsons 1994

ISBN 1 86950 136 5

Designed and typeset by Pages Literary Pursuits
Printed by HarperCollins, Hong Kong

Contents

Acknowledgements

Some of the material reproduced in *Four Seasons of Trout* has appeared previously in *New Zealand Fisherman* and *Rod & Rifle*, and I am most grateful for permission to use it. I am most grateful, also, to several individuals who gladly provided historical and other information, among them Mrs Margaret Potts of South Australia for background information about her father-in-law, Jerry Potts; Gil Brandeis of Wellington for the Hedgehogger trout-fly pattern; Mrs Cassie Blair of Taupo for notes about her father, Greg Kelly; Allan and Barbara Cooper of Tauranga for historical information about the Taupo fishery; Jim McAloon and Bob Bragg of Christchurch for providing new information about W.H. Spackman; and Jim Ackerley of Ashburton for his welcome example to us all.

I must also express my thanks to local historian and C&S Publications Editor Ron Cooke of Taumarunui for his help with information about the golden fishing years of Kakahi. Thanks are also due to the Taupo Fishing Club for permission to reproduce an article from a club publication; to the National Library for its first-class reference services to researchers; to National Archives, Christchurch, for its help in backgrounding something of W.H. Spackman's life in Christchurch; to the Taupo District Museum of Art and History for permission to use information about the Parsons' Glory trout fly from their files; to New Zealand Post for details about an early postmaster, trout-fisher and trout-fly designer, Basil Humphrey; to the *Taupo Times* newspaper for Taupo fishery information from their early files; and to the Department of Conservation for fishery statistics.

My warmest thanks go to my illustrator, Angela Müller, for her admirable drawings, some of which were inspired by historical photographs and illustrations from a variety of sources; and to my editor, Mark Bathurst, for his many improvements to my original text.

J.P.

Preface

I have written another book to please myself. Whenever a trout-fishing episode or subject seems more than usually interesting, I make haste to write about it.

We should all do it! We should all write down what we have seen and heard, and done, and thought about, when fishing. It doesn't matter that we cannot summon the lyricism of a Dana Lamb, an Odell Shepard or a Patrick Chalmers. As long as we do take pen to paper we should just write things down as best we can. Nothing is more enjoyable, later, than re-living the magic of time spent fishing. Bliss suffuses that experience more and more, whatever the misery of some of the original magic. And that's another thing: the angling rough is as much a part of fishing as the angling smooth, and if we write only of the smooth we utterly deceive ourselves, besides robbing our future reading of much of its piquancy.

I write things down while the pictures and the thoughts are still fresh and strong. I go back to those words and wrestle with them again and again, until I know that I am just not capable of making the retelling any better.

Besides writing, my world of fishing is well blessed with other enjoyments: the treasures stored in fishing books; delight in birds (even delight in paradise duck and spur-winged plover, provided they stay mute); the aquatic and terrestrial insects of trout-fishing; the tying of flies; photography; the search for documents revealing information about angling men and angling matters of bygone days.

As one fishes into what the advertising industry euphemistically calls the twilight years, the compulsion to kill fish subsides. And in my case, if not, perhaps, in yours, I don't now want to creep out of bed in the four o'clock dark of a melancholy morning so that I can cast a fly at the first stroke of five. Or even persevere from moonless dusk to darkest midnight, just to increase my chances of catching fish.

So, night-time may be the best time to catch fish, but daytime is the time to go fishing, for fishing is about enjoyment, and nowadays, for me, there's no enjoyment in fishing when I can't see the winter kingfisher in the bare willow, or hear the summer snap of broom pods popping in the noonday heat, or watch trout dashing at smelt in a sparkling rip.

I am lucky to live just a few minutes from still-water fishing, and only an hour or so from river and stream fishing. As I look out of the window now, over Acacia Bay and beyond, three of the big commercial boats are trolling along the sheltered eastern shore between Waitahanui and the White Cliffs, while a chilly southerly drives a sea of whitecaps past them down the lake, and snow showers veil the tops of the Kaimanawas.

I have been fishing twice in the past week and caught nothing, though on the second occasion fish spasmodically broke the calm surface of the bay. They would take nothing I placed in their way. Such indifference impresses humility on one. I went ashore that afternoon and contemplated the wet black sand on the beach, and thought to myself that in the grand scheme of things I was no more than just another grain of sand on an infinity of sandy beach; sometimes with answers about the world of fish and fishing, and sometimes without; and always — always — deeply grateful for the presence of that wonderful world, and all else that springs from it.

My four seasons are not an orderly succession of tales limited to a single year, but a selection from several recent years of angling enjoyments. I like writing about such enjoyments, and hope that you will enjoy them equally with me.

John Parsons
Taupo, 1993

Each season of the year, as it comes round, is the best. Each day,
each hour that we are alive, is the richest. For what is yesterday but a memory,
and what is tomorrow — which may never come?

Robert Gibbings

Spring

Captain Richardson's Pool

I really don't know where I got the idea that the watercolour of Richardson's Pool, on the Waikato River, which hung for some years in the old Taupo Public Library, had been painted by someone called L.W. Johnson.

I think one of the library staff must have kindly climbed up to it for me on a chair and read the artist's name as such. I know I was far more taken with the title of the painting, and the painting itself, than with the identity of the painter; for here was a name which at once took me back to the day I had talked at length with Dr John Armstrong of Taupo about the halcyon years of the Waikato River's trout-fishing, and those extraordinary hatches of sedge flies, and about Alan Pye, and a man called Richardson.

Captain Richardson he was, in fact; one of that trio of quite dissimilar men of the late 1920s who occasionally spent time in one another's company either fishing or talking interminably about stream flies both natural and artificial: Dr Armstrong himself, medical practitioner, leading citizen and keen entomologist; Alan Pye, enigmatic future proprietor of Huka Fishing Lodge; and Captain Richardson, a retired civil engineer and world traveller who spent three years in Taupo sailing and fishing; names now fast fading from the consciousness of local people.

Alan Pye's name will outlive the others'. Dr Armstrong's is now almost forgotten; would that someone in the town who had known him well had written at length of the man and his services to the fledgeling community of Taupo. Captain Richardson had slipped away virtually without trace until I read the title of the painting in the library. True, he did appear in a piece I published elsewhere about the three friends of those Waikato River days.

No-one apart from Dr Armstrong had ever mentioned Captain Richardson to me, although Monty Tisdall was able to describe for me the floating sedge pattern which the Captain designed for the undoing of those big free-rising rainbows of the Waikato downstream of the town. Once upon a time, in the 1930s, Tisdall's had sold the pattern commercially.

Then, quite recently, looking through a copy of the *Taupo Times'* Taupo centennial supplement of 1969, I suddenly caught sight of a name — Captain Arthur Richardson. Jerry Potts, that colourful Taupo wildlife ranger and jack of all trades of the 1920s, was recollecting some of his more memorable experiences.

Dr Armstrong had told me that Richardson's Pool lay a little downstream of Reid's Farm, the riverbank reserve on the way to Huka Lodge from Taupo, and that the Captain liked to fish it "from a high rocky spot there". Like the settings of other landscape paintings and photographs of those days, however, the setting of Richardson's Pool of the 1930s bears no resemblance to the overgrown landscape there of the present day.

The Captain fished his pool whenever he could, delighting in taking from it the heavy rainbow trout of those wonderful days of the late 1920s and early 1930s, when rainbows averaged — averaged, mind you — some 3kg.

Those days were enshrined in a little booklet of 30 pages entitled *Where the Rainbow Rise!*, written by a man called G.W. Johns and published by the Rotorua Post Printing House, presumably between 1930 and 1935 (although one New Zealand authority says 1949). The booklet sought to publicise the quality of the trout-fishing available to anglers visiting the central North Island. It talks glowingly of all the wonderful lake and river-fishing awaiting anglers in the Taupo and Rotorua districts.

I had never been greatly impressed by the quality of the six water colours, painted by the author, which embellish the text of the booklet. True, reproduction of colour in New Zealand in those far-off days was still in its infancy, although I must say that the reproduction of plainly hand-coloured photographs in the 1930 issues of New Zealand's excellent *Wanderlust Magazine* clearly achieved standards far ahead of their time. But not in G.W. Johns' *Where the Rainbow Rise!*, so I had always supposed that Mr Johns was a somewhat mediocre watercolourist.

Now, however, able to examine the signature on the Richardson's Pool painting for myself, I realised with a start that the man who had painted that first-class Waikato River watercolour was G.W. Johns himself.

I wonder where the originals are of the G.W. Johns' watercolours reproduced in *Where the Rainbow Rise!*. There is no reason to suppose that they would have fallen short of the standard so manifest in the Richardson's Pool painting, but, even so, they may well have dropped into the limbo that engulfs so much local art and history.

If the originals have been lost, we are at least left with the tiny, unlovely reproductions in *Where the Rainbow Rise!*. Of course, G.W. Johns himself might not have been too unhappy with the way his paintings were reproduced. After all, here was printed evidence of probably the only publication that would ever appear in his name, and authors and artists do love to see themselves in print.

He was a modest man, I suspect. He wrote knowingly and glowingly of all the best-known fishing rivers and lakes in central North Island rainbow country, and he recommended certain places at which to stay. He singled out Huka Lodge and Alan Pye for special praise. He also mentions a "comfortable little lodge at which to stay" at Atiamuri, where good fish were to be caught, grand wet-fly fishing was to be had, and hatches of iron blue, olives and sedges experienced. He quite forgot to say that the comfortable little lodge in question was owned and run by no less a sportsman, author and painter than G.W. Johns; and although he painted views of the Waiotaka River and Lake Taupo, and no fewer than four of the Waikato River, he studiously avoided the Waikato at Atiamuri in his little book.

In those days, believe it or not, his Atiamuri Fishing Lodge offered 2 miles (3.2km) of private fishing water. The tariff was 15 shillings ($1.50) a day, 5 shillings (50c) less than at Huka Lodge.

If he were alive today and just happened to wander into the Taupo Museum, I think G.W. Johns would smile a little smile of mingled pleasure and pain when he came to the trout-fishing exhibits. The angling paraphernalia of days gone by would kindle happy memories. He would nod as if to say, "I told you so," when confronted by Pye's record 6.1kg trout in its glass case. Then he would see the photographs — of a huge catch of fish, of contemporaries of his, of a dog called Major he had once known, sitting beside its master, Alan Pye, on the riverbank, waiting for the evening rise.

And he would see, with a thrill of pleasure, a suddenly familiar watercolour entitled "Richardson's Pool, Waikato River".

A break at Turangi

Logging trucks swept by in blinding clouds of spray. All the trucks and cars coming through from Turangi had their lights on, and I thought to myself that my three days of freedom were already blighted. George had said the big river was surely going to be dirty. Driving south from his shop at Waitahanui into the darkness and the rain hammering at the car, I had to believe him. I hadn't been away like this for at least a year, and yet, on the morning after as beautiful an early summer day as you could wish for in spring, Fate had turned the tables on me — again. My three days of bliss, fishing the Tongariro, were doomed.

Not so. Crazy mixed-up weather characterised the days I spent in Turangi, but the river refused to succumb to the downpours and stayed clear. True, I once got very wet indeed and had good reason, yet again, to curse my last-but-one waterproof jacket for letting in the rain. It sports a camouflage pattern, this so-called waterproof parka — guaranteed waterproof, incidentally, by the shop where I bought it (or else I wouldn't have taken it).

When it leaked unashamedly the first time, I took it back to the shop. The manufacturers didn't offer to replace it, they merely resealed the seams on the inside. They took an awfully long time to do this remedial work, and my expectations of a really waterproof parka at long last (expectations bolstered by the loving care and attention that was surely being lavished on the jacket during the weeks it was away) grew and grew. I suppose I am naive, but one hopes for the best.

Nothing is more comforting to the angler on a rainy day than remaining snug and dry under a waterproof jacket in a real downpour. I longed for such comfort on the long tramp back from the Cattle Rustlers' Pool to the Major Jones Bridge while a fierce, prolonged rain squall jumped over Pihanga and drenched everything in its path, including me.

When you're wearing a guaranteed-waterproof parka, cold wet patches on neck and shoulders gradually spreading over your skin are no comfort at all. The leaks would have become far more serious had the squall attacked from the other direction, but anyone who, from time to time, takes the lonely walk along that stretch of the Tongariro, will know that the thin screen of manuka and scrub high above the river provides a fair measure of protection in a southerly.

That parka, so attractively finished in green and brown camouflage colours for the outdoorsman, is only one of several I've owned which have let in the rain; but, as I said, it is my last-but-one waterproof jacket. Perhaps I should have worn my latest purchase, but, optimistically, I did not think the weather would be cold enough, and so I left it at home.

I could have done with it twice during my three days of fishing at Turangi. I'll know to take it in future, just in case. It is an English Barbour jacket, waterproof, wind-proof, utterly trustworthy. Heavy in the hand, yes, but you don't notice the weight once you've put it on. I'm greedy for another, the short version designed for wear with chest waders. The one I have is certainly a jacket and not a coat — the hem falls below the tops of thigh boots, but not far below — but of course it is quite unsuitable for wear with chest waders. A short waterproof and wind-proof alternative, for those cold wet days when you nevertheless want to wade deep in chest waders but don't want your jacket dragging in the water, would complement the other jacket superbly. One day . . .?

Change is inseparable from fishing the Tongariro. No matter how much you want the river to remain as it was when you and the world were younger and somehow better rewarded, floods inexorably reshape the watercourse here and there, sometimes for worse, sometimes for better. The Tongariro is not the product of a constant flow of water, but the carrier of tribute from a score of sources, tribute which varies in volume according to rain-fall and snow melt across central North Island valleys and mountains large and small. Change is constant.

This time, fishing the "long walk" side of Judge's on the afternoon of my arrival, I found a shallower pool than before, and encountered nothing at all. Yet perhaps that water is not now entirely abandoned in favour of other places, for only the next evening, when I took downstreaming tackle down the true left bank of Judge's, three anglers occupied that other, "long walk" side of the pool, expectantly fishing into a dusk which, because of the rain we'd had that day, promised a run of fish.

Change persuaded me not to drop down the steep bank to fish the Stag. In the past, a swampy area below the cliff had to be negotiated on the way to that pool. Today, as I saw from the top of the bank, ponded water lay in wait for the unwary. Maybe it wouldn't be at all difficult to find a way through the swamp and the blackberry, but I chose to push on to the Cattle Rustlers'. There again, of course, changes along the river be-tween the Stag and Neverfail pools over the past year or so have been quite dramatic. Possibly no other stretch of the Tongariro has altered so considerably. All the time I have known the river fairly well, almost 20 years, a small bypass river has flowed out of the Stag under the long curv-ing cliff leading to Cunningham's Corner, just below the old Admiral's Pool, where the bypass and the main river came together again at the tail of the long island between them.

Now we are back to the days before the big flood of 1958, for the bypass has become the main river again. I looked longingly down from the cliff on the little bypass pool I called Double Rock, and longed to be able to fish it again. It might be possible to do so, but only if, in chest waders, one can work a way safely upstream under the cliff from Cunningham's Corner.

Cunningham's Corner: now there's a pool that's changed considerably over the past three years. Few may know it as Cunningham's. Keith Gallaugher coined the name Blackberry Pool for it when a new flood enlarged what I knew as the Sallow Pool, which itself lay a couple of hundred metres below Cunningham's. He fished it from the true left bank with a deadly tandem nymph tackle — a heftily weighted size 8 nymph trailing a size 12 white caddis with a black head. The little caddis did the damage. The pool is much bigger now, and very deep along the true right bank. Unhappily, as with other pools on the Tongariro these days, notably Waddell's and the Fan, a substantial eddy complicates fishing it with a nymph.

When I fished it on the morning of my second day, however, I did draw a response from two fish. The deep water flowing under the bank appeared empty, but the eddying water close to the incoming currents plainly held fish. The two that came at the caddis stayed on for a minute or so, and then broke free, I think because the imitation was dressed too far round the bend of the hook, thus allowing too insubstantial a hold.

On the morning of the third day, at half past seven, only two anglers were fishing the Major Jones, and one of those was a heron. No-one at all was fishing the Hydro on my side, although one man stood on top of the rock where the Mangamawhitiwhiti joins the main river, and almost as I arrived he was into a fish, but lost it at the bank a minute or two later. Well, even though I had intended to fish the Neverfail, the luxury of fishing an untenanted Hydro was not to be passed up, and I went in about halfway up, at the point where Frank Schlosser always used to say that the best of the pool began for the nympher.

The morning opened quietly, and grey, and slowly improved into sunshine. The Hydro Pool appeared to be the same old pool I had known for years, but rather more full of water than before — deep still on the western bank — and definitely more promising at the top than I could remember from visits some years before.

Quite soon a fish struck at the nymph, and almost wasn't there when I tried to drive the hook home. I moved a few metres to a generous but shallow pocket of water at the head of the pool, and almost immediately a fish had the nymph, again only briefly.

In earlier years I would have waded grimly up the Boulevard to the Neverfail. Some of the water alongside the scrub overhanging that bank had provided shelter for fish pausing between the Hydro and the Neverfail, and I looked forward to renewing acquaintance with their successors. But more water nowadays comes down that side, as I could see, and I decided not to try conclusions with it on this occasion

Someone had told me that the Neverfail had undergone a dramatic

8

change and that unless the river was low one could not fish the pool as of old. I soon saw why. The little bypass breaking away from the main river some way above the pool had now become a river in its own right. It joined the main stem at the tail of the pool, as before, but in greatly increased measure, making a much narrower island of the one from which I and scores of other anglers had upstreamed or downstreamed that invariably productive pool. Today, strong fast water tearing down under the bank to join up with the main river would have inhibited even the most intrepid angler anxious to get out onto the island alongside the Neverfail Pool we used to know.

I did spot a quiet stretch just below the junction of the waters downstream of the island, and I managed to find a way through the scrub and down the bank below the stretch, convinced that here was a piece of water that would yield at least a present-day limit of three unwary fish. Fond hope! Nothing was home there, for cast after cast after cast, and I came away mystified by my failure.

Three nymphers were fishing the Hydro when I went back to it, but none of them showed any signs of wanting to fish the upper half of the pool, so I started in where I'd begun much earlier, and was very quickly playing a fish and losing it. That made three I had lost that morning in the Hydro. The next one stayed on. I was so sure it was a small fish that I tried to bustle it into the bank before the other three anglers could see what I had, but it wasn't all that small. In fact it weighed 1.5kg, an average-size Taupo trout, and it took five minutes to land and knock on the head.

The previous day's two encounters, and that day's four, had all come in the morning. Nothing took any interest in the afternoon. That was also the experience of another angler I met, who had hooked eight fish in three days, and all of them before midday. His afternoons had been devoid of fish. It was not altogether surprising, then, that the afternoon of my third day at Turangi should prove utterly blank.

I felt betrayed by this indifference, not simply because I caught no fish, but because I caught no fish *along Boulder Reach*, a favourite stretch which had hardly ever failed to produce a fish or two for me in the past. I actually felt doubly betrayed, because it had taken an effort of will to drive south out of Turangi and leave the car at the Red Hut car park, scene of so many recent car break-ins. I so wanted to fish upstream of the Red Hut Pool, especially Boulder Reach, that I decided to risk leaving the car. No other cars were there when I arrived, but another one pulled in a few minutes after me. The two fishermen in it were as aware as I was of the risk we were

9

taking. They parked even closer to the highway than I had done. Only four or five years ago, broken windscreens and resultant thefts from parked cars throughout the district were unthinkable. Nowadays they are all too common, reflecting social problems which, while the economy remains depressed, will show no signs of diminishing.

Incidence of theft from anglers' cars has wrought considerable change within the Taupo fishery. Coupled with a recent dearth of fish there (and a coincidental feast of large fish at Rotorua), the problem of theft has kept many fishermen away. Those who do come often leave their cars at the motel and walk to their fishing, a practice which of course won't do them any harm at all. Favourite waters some distance from anglers' accommodation are not now fished as heavily as they were, but some moteliers are obligingly taking clients to and from those more distant pools.

On that third afternoon, glumly finishing up without a touch at the top of Boulder Reach, I decided to carry on up to the Fan. If the car was going to get broken into I could do nothing about it anyway, at this distance, and another hour away from it was not going to make any difference.

That hour at the Fan proved utterly unrewarded, and I might just as well have made my way back to the car when I had finished at Boulder Reach. Swallows wove intricate patterns of flight over the pool, two subdued paradise ducks flew grandly past low over the water, and all of a sudden a wind sprang up, and out of the southeastern Kaimanawas rain came pelting across the pool out of a livid sky. This fisherman got wet again, although not as wet as the day before.

It was a relief to get back to the car and find it just as I had left it, quite safe and sound.

Next day I took the long way home to Taupo, stopping off at Kuratau to fish first the rivermouth and then the sandspit. What a restful, dreamy, faintly sunny early morning it was at the rivermouth! No fish showed; no smelt appeared; a pair of black swans, a pair of red-billed gulls and a pair of paradise duck pottered peacefully about. But no trout came to the lure I swung time and again across the faint rip.

Then two station wagons arrived on the beach 400 metres away. Parents and children leapt out and busied themselves launching an aluminium boat from a trailer. Soon an outboard motor was shattering the peace of the morning, but much worse was to follow. The party had also brought a water bike or jet ski. Naturally, with the compulsion that urges the drivers of Jaguar cars to pass everything else on the road, the riders of jet skis are compelled to make as much noise and as much spray as possible.

It's strange how some people are utterly oblivious of everyone else's well-being, yet are always the first to complain if someone invades their own privacy. Perhaps they think they are doing the rest of the world so obviously within earshot a favour by generously sharing their surfeit of decibels.

Typically, commercial radio frenzy blared from one of the cars. Later, at the sandspit, trying to shut out the obscene noise of the jet ski from my enjoyment of the morning, I was interested to see a local launch pull round and come alongside the obscenity after its rider had once again fallen off. Words were said by the launch owner, the jet ski and its rider went ashore and did not venture out again. I supposed the question of the speed limit within 200 metres of the shore had been invoked.

I wonder if these monstrous machines would still appeal to the adolescents who drive them if they made no noise at all?

Spring's here!

Everything fell happily into place this afternoon. We have so long been starved of sunshine that warm spring weather is doubly welcome. Today the sun shone, and breezes blew faintly from somewhere between southeast and southwest, depending on where you were at the time; and a couple of sturdy fish came to the fly.

Watching the wavelets sweeping into Acacia Bay below, and the far narrow bands of calm water nestling under the shores of Rotongaio and Hatepe, I knew that the eastern shore of Whakaipo would be calm, so I drove confidently there after lunch, nodding at the evidence of spring adorning so much of the land on the way, such as the new, rust-coloured leaves of the big grove of poplars on the crest of the valley overlooking Robertson's farm, the lambs in the paddocks, and then, at Whakaipo, the medicinal scent of sun-warmed pine-needles, the scent that at once transported me back 50 years to the dry, sun-bathed, pine-hung banks of the lakes at Keston.

But I might have known that what's true of wind direction in one place isn't necessarily true of wind direction in another place only a handful of kilometres away, even if lines drawn on maps conclusively demonstrate that the wind here must blow from precisely the same quarter as the wind there.

I never learn. I am an incurable optimist. Time and time again I examine the wind and the waves animating the lake and the land below us in Acacia Bay, and promptly draw conclusions which so often bear no resemblance to the reality greeting me elsewhere.

It was the same again today, but not as dramatically and inhospitably the same as on some of the occasions at Whakaipo I've known throughout this past winter. I expected the northeastern side of the bay to offer shelter, and to a certain extent it did, but for much of the time I fished into a breeze which surely came straight across from Western Bay. Luckily, it wasn't the big wind that heaves long waves so boisterously along that if you want to wade deep you have to jump up and over the more aggressive of them. It was a slight breeze. Though mostly from the west, it carried a hint of the snow I could see piled high on the Tongariro National Park mountains to the south, but, glory be, I actually fished without a jacket for the first time in months.

Waves glittered in the sun, and a kingfisher called, and a heron sailed ponderously past. Somewhere near among the new green skirts of the willows, a bellbird called, and I called back, and it called again, and I

called back again, and this went on for some time. The exchange might have lasted indefinitely, but a fish fastened on to the green Hairy Dog, and in my excitement I forgot about being a bellbird. It wasn't a big fish. All the same, it was a rainbow jack suddenly wanting to become much better acquainted with the mouth of the bay as a first stop on the way to Turangi. He would have weighed no more than 1.5kg, but battled doggedly right to the end, and scuttled off when I released him.

That fish came five minutes after I had delivered my first cast. I don't like fish to come so soon, and I wasn't going to like the next hour of nothing at all. Not even a tiddler came. No fish troubled the fly, but the bellbird and I whistled to each other, and the breeze waxed and waned, and a quail called raucously quite close.

No trout voluntarily broached anywhere that I could see, the whole time I was there, and no smelt or bully swam thereabouts. Often, when the waves undulate past, and smelt are about, they will gather on your downwind side, as though you're a rock. But not today.

Sheepishly, after the unrewarded hour of casting, I bolstered my flagging optimism by inviting thoughts of the savage strikes I would have in another 10 metres. For there was The Hotspot, and The Hotspot so often saves the day, doesn't it? I took off the Hairy Dog and knotted on a little Red Setter.

The lake level was ideal. It has dropped a few inches over past days, and I could now wade out a little further, which meant the clutching hands of the willows couldn't quite reach the fly on the back cast. If only the lake would stay the way it was today! Only a little washed-up weed lay along the shore. The water came in clean and bright to the stony beaches.

Birds came and went. Three black swans flew in majestically, lowering their big black paddles to skim the surface and brake their landing speed. A kingfisher arrowed to a fishing perch in a willow. I could not remember seeing one here while the lake was low. Do they forsake places like this when the water recedes some way from trees which would normally overhang it?

Third cast at The Hotspot, a strong fish took hold of the Red Setter and rushed it away for 20 metres before jumping out into the sunlight and showing me a fine, deep side. It was a most splendid and acrobatic fish, and I thought if I managed to land it I would keep it. I did land it, and later it weighed a little under 2kg on the kitchen scales. Smoked, it will suitably enhance the attractions of Lake Taupo for one or other of the sets of visitors we're expecting over the summer months.

New light on Parsons' Glory

Angling history is continually unfolding. We did not know until the mid-1950s that dear old Izaak Walton had, by our standards, shamelessly pirated an earlier fishing book than his and plundered it of the device of dialogue, and certain of the content, for himself. The reputation he had enjoyed for his *Compleat Angler* for just on 300 years suffered somewhat in consequence thereafter.

And until, in 1978, Dr Donald Scott of Otago University and two fellow researchers from California demonstrated Sonoma Creek origins for our rainbow trout in New Zealand, we had been led to believe, ever since 1924, that they had come from the Russian River.

Even the history of some New Zealand trout flies — a matter of no great importance to those who are not trout-fishers, but of considerable interest to those who are — is destined never, perhaps, to be finally settled.

You might think that nothing more could ever be said that hasn't been said already about that remarkably effective trout fly called Parsons' Glory. Keith Draper tells the story of the fly's origins in his definitive work *Trout Flies in New Zealand*. That was in 1971.

More information has now come to light, in the form of a single, un-dated, typewritten sheet of paper found in the files of the Taupo District Museum of Art and History. The folk at the museum have no idea where the information came from, but it appears to be quite genuine.

Our unknown authority says that Philip Parsons, the originator of the fly named after him, was introduced to Lake Taupo trout-fishing between 1918 and 1920. Contrary to the claims of various trout-fishing authors, says our writer, Parsons was neither an English parson nor a Te Awamutu farmer: he was a New Zealander who farmed at Meeanee and Poraite, near Napier. Before he made his first visit to Taupo he was already fishing the Tutaekuri River, which, prior to the Napier earthquake in 1931, flowed past his farm at Meeanee.

Joe Edmondson, an old fishing companion who managed the Acetone Company in Napier, is believed to have been responsible for Phil Parsons' first visit to Taupo. The pair used to stay at the Terraces Hotel (now De Brett's), where they ate trout for breakfast and tea. The days were spent fishing the Waitahanui River from the Lady's Pool down to the highway bridge.

About 1923, when the Clarks of Eskdale auctioned off their land on the lakefront at Taupo, Edmondson and Parsons bought adjoining sections for £50 ($100.00) each. Both sections were later absorbed into the property on which Twin Peaks Lakeside Inn — formerly first La Vista Motels, and then La Vista Royale Motor Inn — now stands. Our unknown writer says that Phil Parsons spent all his holidays for the remainder of his life at the cottage he built on his Taupo section.

Although he was already making the Parsons' Glory fly in 1924 — a fly he devised himself to suit the particular needs of the Waitahanui River — it was not named officially until 1928. During its first four years the reputation of the Parsons' Glory grew and grew — spread, no doubt, by the praises of Parsons' Waitahanui fishing companions, Ross, Edmondson, Branson, Lane, MacLean and Daley.

In the late 1920s, demand for the fly prompted Ronald Crowther, owner of the Lake Front Store, to have it tied commercially by Tisdall's in Auckland. When Crowther received the first consignment he approached Parsons and asked him whether the fly could be named the Parsons' Glory. Permission was given. The fly quickly moved into legend.

Not long after it had been named, Jimmy Ross "patented" a fly of his own, the Tiger Ross (now more familiar as the Taupo Tiger), which has also since moved into legend. Ross, a great friend of Parsons, owned the only sports shop in Napier at the time. (Incidentally, it was he who donated the Ross Shield for schoolboy rugby.) A rare photograph, taken by the old *Auckland Weekly* in the late 1930s, shows Jimmy Ross admiring an 8½lb (3.8kg) trout held up by Philip Parsons.

The biggest trout Parsons ever landed was a 15½lb (7kg) rainbow which he caught fishing off the spit on the town side of the wharf. Word got around that Mr Parsons had hooked a big one and an audience gathered to watch him play and land it.

How does the present-day Parsons' Glory compare with the original, asks our writer? Although the current pattern retains the original shape, it no longer uses the original feather. Today, he says, the neck feathers of the golden bantam are used, whereas Parsons used the neck feathers of a Barred Rock rooster.

Now that is most interesting. A Barred Rock rooster is the same as a Plymouth Rock rooster, which is noted among fly-tiers for grizzle, or grizzly, hackles — pale feathers barred along their length with much darker marks; so the original Parsons' Glory was winged with a grizzle feather from a Plymouth Rock rooster.

15

But hold on. The various authorities on fly-dressing say that grizzle feathers are white barred with black. Did Phil Parsons tie his masterpiece with white feathers barred with black? I don't think so, for I have in front of me an example of a Parsons' Glory which, I am assured, is an exact replica of the original. It was tied on a size 4 hook by Phil Parsons' son Sam, who very kindly sent it to me in 1977.

The wing is undoubtedly a grizzle feather, but in common with all natural grizzle feathers it combines light and dark browns rather than true whites and blacks. It seems that, unless a pure grizzle turns up, you must always qualify the generic word "grizzle" with an appropriate shade, like red, honey or ginger.

I have mentioned Sam Parsons' fly elsewhere and explained why it was finally considered, here in Taupo, to be a Dorothy and not a Parsons' Glory. I think now that I may have done Sam Parsons an injustice. Even though the two patterns closely resemble each other and were both designed by Phil Parsons, it seems most unlikely that Sam would have confused the two, but I am still not sure.

What we have from Sam is a fly which differs from the contemporary version in both colour and content. Sam's grizzle feathers (there are two, tied in back to back) are a cooler colour than those used today, and the body is the yellow of lupin rather than of broom. These days, a few iridescent greenish-yellow strands, with a suggestion of red about them, flow back from the heads of this and other streamer flies. The strands would be a lot less expensive now than the jungle-cock "eyes" tied in as cheeks on Sam's fly. In the early days, as Keith Draper put it in *Trout Flies in New Zealand*, "no-one would think of tying a fly without using jungle-cock".

It is a pity that our anonymous historian did not describe the original tie in full. He was chiefly concerned to point out the difference in the wing feather colour of today. He mentioned nothing else.

I wonder what he would have made of the photographs of two patterns of the Parsons' Glory, and one of the Dorothy, in Draper's book? And what would Sam have made of them?

Sadly for Sam, the Dorothy in the book is dressed in the cooler colours of the fly he tied for me. Like Sam's — and not surprisingly in a lady — it sports no beard, but unlike Sam's it boasts no jungle-cock eyes, whereas both the photographs of the Parsons' Glories do.

Strangely, although I can see quite well why Sam's fly, apart from the jungle-cock, was earlier pronounced a Dorothy, I don't understand why neither of the Parsons' Glories — either Budge Hintz's tie, or the modern tie illustrated — appears the possessor of grizzle hackles, whereas the Dorothy does. Draper says of the Parsons' Glory that a lot of its success depends on the well-marked honey grizzle feather used for the wing. "Next time you hook a fingerling trout, take a good look at his sides before you tenderly release him and you will see the parr blotches along his side, just like a well-marked honey grizzle feather."

You shouldn't have been here yesterday

Why wasn't it like this yesterday? Yesterday the rain fell and a bitter wind blew. Both rain and wind were a hangover from the drunken spree winter staged at the very end of September to blight our hopes for a fine Opening Day on the first of October. By Friday, two days before the great occasion, spring was smiling warmly on the land. It has been a long cold winter for us, but at last we had turned the corner. Someone reported the river low and clear. That would be a change for Opening Day. The water would still be too cold yet to wade wet, much too cold in fact. We would fish it, Bill and I, in waders. Hurrah for October the first!

I didn't like the way the big day opened. A fine drizzle drifted down from an overall-grey sky. The air was suddenly cold. One of the first signs of prolonged rain hereabouts is the faint, fine drizzle which thickens, and thickens, and keeps on keeping on. That's how it was on Saturday, too. By midday I was already thinking that the low clear river of our expectations just might have to be consigned to the drawerful of dashed Opening Day hopes that most of us have got sadly tucked away somewhere.

Snow closed the Desert Road around midday. The road was reopened in the afternoon (a friend came through by car), but very soon yesterday, Opening Day, it was closed once more. Snow also fell all across the land east of Taupo. Looking out over the lake, we watched the pale grey snow showers drifting eerily over a dark grey landscape.

Today, Monday, blue sky and white cloud has smiled in all directions. The faint southerly breeze, which grew warmer as the day progressed, sank to a zephyr. The contrast between the two days, yesterday and today, is unbelievable. True, our experience of yesterday's malevolence played itself out in the eastern ranges, but no more than 35km from Taupo itself, where conditions appeared benign by comparison when we finally got back to it.

Only a matter of 10km from town snow lay in patches here and there. Distant hills stood up capped with unfamiliar white. We'd come, Bill and I, because in Taupo the weather certainly appeared to be improving. A watery sun showed now and again. Would the weatherman's promises be fulfilled?

As we drove east the day deteriorated. We have gone out on some pretty bad Opening Days before, but never one like this. Water lay in dips and hollows all along the road, and filled the shallow roadside runnels. Snow shone at the southern foot of each telephone pole. The only bird I saw all afternoon displayed what at first I took to be a handful of snow on its back, but it was only a magpie. Rain beat at us all the time. Out in the sodden paddocks new lambs nuzzled and grazed.

Suddenly we were looking down the incline to the Matea Road swamp. It had become the biggest lake I have ever seen there. Away beyond the ripples, snow blanketed the south-facing hills between us and the river, a sight neither of us had seen before.

Upstream of the big waterfall, a streaming valley battered by rain awaited us. We were still prepared to fish — until we saw the river. It was in high flood, a chocolate-brown torrent. This place of snow and rain and roaring waters, and brooding hills drained of colour, bore not the slightest resemblance to the joyful summer place in which I stalked trout not so very long ago.

We negotiated the gullying pumice road with care. Only one new slip posed any kind of challenge for the four-wheel drive, and we eased our way over that without trouble. We turned at the one-car park, went back over the slip, and parked in the pouring rain at the side of the track to toast the new season. Bill made a snowball while I broached the celebratory bottle of wine. I had brought a bottle which did not offend fish or fishing on this day of wild weather. It was neither Dry Fly nor Forellenwein, just plain old moreish Chasseur.

Somewhat lighter in heart for having performed the ritual, we drove up out of the upper valley and headed east into the lower valley. No snow had fallen there, but many hours of rain had obviously made up for it. Down at the new bridge where the Mokomokonui River joins the Waipunga, angry brown waters swept east. It was bad enough yesterday, so what can it have been like there four years ago, when the Waipunga took the old bridge out on its rampaging way to the Mohaka River, 6 metres higher than normal? We shook our heads and drove west to the Tarawera Tavern, where a log fire and double whiskies warmed us through, priming us for the journey back.

Notwithstanding the raging brown waters, the driving rain and the thawing snow patches, we did indeed fish on Opening Day 1990. We fished with Brian Clarke, John Goddard and Hugh Falkus from the comfort of Bill's armchairs at home. The two videos, Goddard's and Clarke's *The Educated Trout* and Falkus's *Salmo — the Leaper*, were delightful, especially on such a day; the one full of the quiet charm of English south-country chalk streams and the leisurely outwitting of brown and rainbow trout by two acknowledged masters of the art of fly-fishing; the other set in Cumbria and Scotland among wilder rivers, wilder scenery and bigger fish, sea trout and salmon.

So it was that we fished vicariously in the morning with some of the world's best, while the southeasterly drove the rain against the windows. Then, because the weatherman said the day would improve, we went out to turn armchair fishing into reality, and came sadly back, again unfulfilled. But there will be other days.

Blackberry Pool

Willows newly green and kowhai newly gold greeted an exploratory trip to the Tongariro. Exploratory? Well, I would be exploring upriver from the Major Jones Bridge. What you know of the river like the back of your hand one week washes down into memory with the next flood, and I would be finding out where this and that pool had disappeared, and finding new pools; and all as a result of the second big flood of the year.

New leaves and blossom, the first shining cuckoo calling and swallows gathering mud from puddles, confirmed that we do have another spring, which is a comfort in these environmentally damaged times.

Maybe, like me, you don't like willows overmuch, but how refreshing they all looked in their new green finery today! I marvel twice each year at that huge and straggling conglomeration of willows and sallows along the last few kilometres of highway into Turangi; first in the cold and frosty heart of winter when the bare branches glow with colours varying from bright yellow to deepest claret; then again in spring, when all the many different varieties there sink their differences and mantle every supple limb and twig in the same shade of lively green.

Someone in Turangi told me I should fish the area until recently occu-

19

pied by the old Admiral's Pool. Yes, the pool itself was no more, and yes, the main course of the river had now returned to the bypass coming down under the curving cliff from the tail of the Stag Pool to the end of the substantial island below; resuming, in fact, the channel it had held to for many years up to the time of the disastrous flood of 1958.

I took the advice I was given readily enough, but I wish now that I had followed my own inclination to explore the other bank — that is, to walk up the true right bank from the Major Jones Bridge — for I found no attractive water on my side except the almost unchanged stretch above the Stag. True, the head of the Stag Pool itself looks promising enough, and it will certainly hold running fish briefly; but, like the Millrace just above the Stag, it appeared to hold nothing today — nothing, at least, that I could interest.

But — and it's a but which looms larger the more I think of it — the pool I saw when I arrived, and so much wanted to fish, lay across the river. Isn't it always so? As I stood contemplating the enjoyment I would soon take from exploring the succession of small pools which I had been told

now lay along a stretch of braided river between the old Admiral's and the Stag, I suddenly saw an angler over the river playing a fish. What a nerve! That pool took on an even greater charm.

It is the pool which was formed some years ago below the tail of the island downstream of the Stag. The water running out of it turns right to tumble down to the Neverfail Pool and then the Boulevard. At one stage, years ago I'm told, anglers knew the area as Gun Club Reach. I gave the little pool at the tail of the reach the name Sallow Pool, and fished it very successfully indeed. Then came the flood of 1985, and a big deep pool formed there which the late Keith Gallaugher of Taupo may have been the first to find. He called it the Blackberry Pool and fished it from the true left bank with a deadly combination of nymphs: a size 8, heavily weighted something-or-other with a size 12, unweighted, black-headed white caddis on a link of tippet looped to the bend of the larger hook. It was the small caddis wavering in the current that did the damage.

I fished the Blackberry Pool once from the other side with Nick, who fastened onto a powerful fish which headed off unstoppably downstream and round the corner.

Today, from the true left bank, the pool looked as though it will become a firm favourite (if it isn't already) — fished from the true right bank, of course — and not only because of its looks, and deeps, but also because it appears to have developed a far less intimidating exit at the tail end.

I decided to fish it, from that side, very soon. But not today. Today I fished it up from my side. Although the main run down the pool tends towards the left bank, the occasional fish will certainly lie there, if not as many as will lie in deeper water comfortably fished from the other side. I struck just one fish, but the encounter was all too brief.

Otherwise, exploring and nymphing up the braided small waters and the enormous new expanse of the Stag, and on to the Millrace, I was aware of only two fish. Both lay on new redds. I saluted them and passed them by, hoping that the next flood would neither stifle their progeny under a thick layer of silt, nor sweep the helpless fry to the lake too soon.

Whakaipo magic

An old-fashioned whistling wind blew the first day, briskly driving waves along the Whakaipo shore. It came straight off the snow-capped mountains of Tongariro National Park.

But the sun tempered the chill in the wind. In the sun on the sheltered shore, Alex and I sweltered with welcome cups of tea mid-morning.

Already, several fish had come Alex's way. I don't think he has ever done so well so quickly at Whakaipo before, yet here is a fishery supposedly teetering on the brink of disaster. People, including Alex, are either predicting doom and gloom for Taupo trout-fishers, or insisting that remedial measures are essential if the place is to continue to justify the reputation of its principal sporting attraction.

He landed eight fish in the first two hours, four in the first hour, four in the second, while I, the resident angler, had to make do with four encounters, only two of which translated into landed fish, just one of which I kept. But the day radiated magic. There was a fresh, clean wash of water continuously on the shore, fussing and fossicking among rocks and flotsam free from the putrefaction of rotting weed upon the beach. They'll come again, the mounds of washed-up weed, in winter, when the lake sinks lower and lower, and our hearts with it. But before then, not far away from October, if strong winds blow when new weed growth is a-springing, we'll have an early harvest of green weeds upon the shore which might last some weeks.

Stepping between the rocks along the shoreline as we made our way to Willow Point, we came across a pathetic little bundle of pale, soft feathers half-hidden in the wrack of weed and sticks thrown up by the waves. Out in the bay, three of the little bird's living siblings paddled expectantly between their black swan parents, who delved for weed to feed the depleted family.

Only one other small cloud crossed the smiling face of Whakaipo that day (for me, anyway) — a single spur-winged plover whose screeching complaint flew about from above like a shrill firecracker.

Lambs cried from the paddocks. Kingfishers batted territorial messages across to one another. Most of the shags one normally sees at Whakaipo were plainly on compassionate leave somewhere else. A shining cuckoo called, the first I have heard this year at Taupo. Waxeyes wandered, companionably piping, through the fresh green leaves of the willows curtseying here and there along the shore. And broom bushes bubbled over with a riot of yellow blooms.

The second day was so much like the first that the two of them fuse together in my mind. I know only that Alex continued to catch fish while I did not — well, barely. Trout magic touched him more often than it touched me, but we were both enchanted by the wonders of another Whakaipo spring so generously revealed.

Once again, though, I saw no smelt or bullies active in the shallows. One dead bully lay cushioned by shoreline flotsam. Five or six half-digested smelt did certainly float on the surface at one stage. They marked the departure of yet another trout Alex returned to the lake. It had disgorged the smelt. It had probably disgorged more smelt while Alex was playing it, for the ones it left behind close to the shore plainly occupied a fairly early place in the queue of food on its way through that fish, but there was no sign of more recent food that we could see. It's strange, but although I have written briefly elsewhere about the phenomenon of regurgitated food, instancing both Captain J.S. Phillips' and John H. Roush Jnr's experiences, I had never before seen evidence of regurgitation myself.

Another most unusual sight at Whakaipo, but one hardly calculated to send any but the participants into raptures, was the occasional presence on shoreline rocks of ladybirds busily engaged in ensuring a future for their species.

Three weeks later, ladybirds still crawled about the shore and mated here and there — I counted 10 of the little beetles on one rock — yet my recollection of the day, many years ago now, when I happened upon a similar collection of ladybirds on a stunted hebe at Whakamoenga, and photographed the group, was that it was a midsummer day, hot, windy, parched, with the sunlight almost blinding in its intensity. It would surely have been the wrong time of year for that to have been a mating occasion too?

Smelting fever

When Roy alerted us to the presence of smelt, the gloom lifted. We might now catch a fish or two.

We were a foursome anxious for action, but only Alex and I had so far taken a fish. Mine had come to an Orange Rabbit fished deep through the sheltered water on the southern shore of the spit at Kuratau. It was anything but a record-breaking rainbow, a slim silver hen of little more than a kilogram, but it was my first of the trip, and — who was to know? — might just be the last.

Three other morning anglers were there before us, fishing that southern shore, when we arrived in the early light a little after 6 o'clock. They were as anxious as we were to see the morning repeat the previous early morning's generosity, when at least 10 fish had come ashore. But that morning's water had lain stained and sullen in the bay curling round to the south, the aftermath of hours of heavy rain in the hills. The downpour had hardly cheered our party, three of whom had come from the other end of the North Island. A fishing holiday is so much more enjoyable at Taupo in fine weather. Even so, in swelling and becoming noticeably brown, the river had brought down food, or the appearance of food, and trout went hunting into the murk and found Yellow Rabbits and Parsons' Glories among the natural titbits. Ten or 12 of the hunters came kicking convulsively ashore.

Today, however, the river ran clear. Waves rounding the spit rolled in from the north. When you looked across to Stump Bay and Motuoapa, a rosy sky behind patches of dark cloud told you that the sun had risen over the hills out there. Only one landed fish enlivened the scene, although Alex later took another from the shallows just north of the spit, and lost a couple too. Then Roy appeared on the scene. He had been trying the mouth of the river to catch his first Lake Taupo trout. In the quiet eddying waters there, small groups of smelt swam slowly about, he said.

After breakfast, Alex and I walked hopefully down to the mouth of the river. In those same quiet eddying waters, a trout rose. Alex cast to it and hooked it. I waded the 50 metres across current to the left-hand edge of the rip. A trout golloped at the surface, and I cast to it; the line pulled tight, I struck, and the hook came away. I said something short and sharp.

The next one, or the one after, stayed on. I waded back over the river, landed the quite respectable 1.5kg jack fish, and heeled a grave for it in the black sand. I was so thrilled by the presence of smelting fish, and so anxious to get back to them at the rip, that I couldn't understand why the fly was caught in something under the sand. Idiot. I had killed and buried the fish without releasing the fly from its jaw. I looked around guiltily, saw no-one except Alex 30 metres away, dug up the fish and took out the fly.

Luckily for us, no-one else came to share the brief bounty of the rip with us for at least half an hour. We enjoyed occasionally heart-stopping and continuously expectant fishing for an hour. Nothing in my trout-fishing experience is quite as stimulating as hungrily-smelting fish at a Lake Taupo rivermouth. I was luckier than Alex. To start with, I had fortuitously chosen the side of the rip where there were more fish; and I was fishing a floating line, which seemed better adapted to the conditions than Alex's sinker. I would send the line out virtually parallel with the angle of the rip and let it swing round, occasionally teasing the fly jerkily towards me. Trout after trout came greedily to it. They pulled fiercely at it, and ran and jumped repeatedly, which is the way of hooked trout in shallow water. I must have encountered 10 fish in the hour we were there, and I had six of them on for varying amounts of time, chiefly very short. Three of the six stayed on the hook, and I knocked them on the head to take home.

In some ways the occasion resembled a time long ago when Alex and I fished the Whanganui rip together and proudly took 18 rainbows. Sometimes the sun shone then, as it did this day, skipping brilliant reflections from the waves. Sometimes cloud came across. All those years ago no boats trolled past, but they did on this occasion, and the anglers aboard them became mere silhouettes against the brilliant light. Behind us on the beach a couple of black-billed gulls walked thoughtfully about, just as they'd done years ago. But at Kuratau we didn't finish up with 18 fish.

I wonder now, two days later, whether we would have killed the 16 we were legally entitled to take had they come unceasingly to the fly. I think we probably would have, despite all the talk of greatly diminished numbers of fish in the lake. Smelting fever is thoroughly contagious.

Trio of Hobbses

I like to think that the English trout-fisher A. Edward Hobbs was related to the trout-fishing Hobbs brothers of Christchurch — Geoffrey and Derisley.

All three loved their trout-fishing. Two of them, Edward and Geoffrey, wrote memorably of their sport, Edward in 1946 and Geoffrey in 1955. Derisley, on the other hand, wrote no less memorably about the fish themselves. Sadly for many of us, especially for Geoffrey, who urged his brother to write about his enjoyment of fishing too, Derisley published only technical and scientifc material. He became an expert in his chosen fields of natural reproduction of salmonids and fisheries management.

After almost 30 years of practical study, investigation and advisory work in New Zealand, Derisley Hobbs accepted an appointment in Tasmania as the chairman of the newly created Inland Fisheries Commission. He died there only two years later, in the early 1960s. His careful, detailed research of earlier years is embodied in three Marine Department publications, *Fisheries Bulletin* numbers 6, 8 and 9, the most important of which was the last, published in 1948, *Trout Fisheries in New Zealand: their development and management*. It has become a classic of fisheries management, just as K. Radway Allen's study of the Horokiwi Stream trout became a classic following its publication in 1951. Interestingly, while Hobbs demonstrated that the natural reproduction of trout was more efficient than propagation in hatcheries, Allen showed that, despite Hobbs' findings, high mortality rates in the initial years among wild trout were an inevitable accompaniment of the natural reproduction process. Both worked for the Freshwater Fisheries Division of the old Marine Department, Hobbs latterly on administration and advisory work, Allen on research.

In 1984, the then assistant director of MAF's freshwater fisheries research group, Bob McDowall, wrote of Hobbs' 1948 classic:

This important bulletin established the foundation upon which the management of New Zealand's trout fisheries has been based for about 40 years, and is a *must* for anyone seriously interested in the subject. It should be compulsory reading for Acclimatisation Society councillors!

Geoffrey Hobbs' freshwater game fish studies were no less thorough than Derisley's, but he conducted his with a fishing rod only. An architect by profession, he spent most of his life, from 1930, in England, returning on fishing holidays to New Zealand from time to time. Those visits, augmented by memories of his youthful fishing, provided the material for an excellent New Zealand book, *Fisherman's Country*, published in 1955. Eight years were to elapse before the appearance of the next general book of New Zealand fishing, Temple Sutherland's *Maui and Me* (which wasn't confined to trout-fishing anyway), so *Fisherman's Country* enjoyed a considerable following, and rightly so; it is a well-written, helpful and wide-ranging survey of the New Zealand trout-fishing experience of that time. Understandably, one reads it now with envy for the better fishing of those days.

Geoffrey wrote an article in 1930 for New Zealand's *Wanderlust* magazine, the high-quality equivalent at the time of our present-day *New Zealand Geographic*. It speaks exuberantly of an idyllic Lake Taupo fishing holiday camped at Motutere Bay with Monty Tisdall; a holiday which preceded his departure for England that same year.

Well before the end of his working life, Geoffrey Hobbs had established himself as a sought-after architect in the West End of London. He was a member of the Fly-fishers' Club, fished for both salmon and trout, became a painter of note and finally retired to Weston-Super-Mare to be close to the lake-fishing he so enjoyed at Blagdon.

I wrote to Geoffrey Hobbs in July 1989, asking him whether he was related to Edward Hobbs, the famous trout-fisher of the River Thames. I ought to have written earlier. By the time my letter reached him he was virtually beyond answering. He died in August, at age 85.

Both Derisley and Geoffrey took an overall view of fish and fishing, but the Englishman Edward Hobbs concentrated on just one river and one species — the River Thames and its big but thinly spread brown trout. He wrote a book of instruction and reminiscence entitled *Trout of the Thames*, published in 1946.

According to the experts of his day, no man was better qualified to catch Thames trout or write about them. His friend Patrick Chalmers — himself an unusually talented angler — called him The Best Thames Angler Ever, a sentiment echoed by another famous angler and writer of those times, Hugh Tempest Sheringham.

Because few trout of the Thames ever responded to a hatch of fly, Thames trout-fishers chose to fish chiefly the spun natural or artificial bait in imitation of the small fry on which the big trout lived. Spinning a bleak or a wagtail might not have been Derisley's or Geoffrey's way with trout, but they would have understood, and been glad to claim kinship with another good keen man of the same name. They surely must have been related!

Good to be alive!

When I came suddenly into view down the track, two paradise ducks and their four small ducklings scuttled furiously for their lives into the lake from the Mapara Stream mouth just a few metres below me. Lugubrious honking from the drake, and hysterical screaming from the duck, conveyed their absolute horror at having been caught so utterly unawares.

The sun shone from a cloudless sky. Snow lay generously on the mountains. Wavelets rippled into the shore all around me, driven by a brisk southwesterly breeze. So what should I do? Should I forget about photography? Although no fish broached, the bay beckoned the fisherman in me invitingly. But I could always take some photographs and then leave the camera gear in the shade under a willow and go back to the car for a rod.

I would walk along the shore with camera and tripod, and I would keep my eyes open for more than photographic subjects. Earlier, on radio, two men had been reported overdue from a boating trip. Their damaged aluminium dinghy had been found in Whakaipo Bay. Away in the western distance, under the forbidding rock walls dropping steeply into the lake, I could just make out a boat or two. Perhaps they were searching the shoreline for the two men?

My own search, for photographic subjects, was rewarded with herons, brilliant orange lichens on dark rocks, three guzzling bumblebees on a single huge purple thistle-head, clusters of nervous shags with eel-like heads, bright, flat sandstone outcrops wet and dry, and the occasional splendour of snowy mountains glittering from the far south.

On such a day it was good to be alive. I walked on and on, over those interminable rocks, right out to the mouth of the bay, while the sun grew in strength and the cool breeze moderated.

Out there, where the bay begins, green beetles flew clumsily everywhere, released into flight by the warm sunshine and the diminishing breeze.

They clung to the rusty-brown banks of rushes on the shore, blundered into trees and rocks, fell helplessly into the shallow miniature lagoons encroaching on that eastern shoreline.

One of the little lagoons, fed by a tiny stream coming out of the swamp that hides behind a dense barrier of rushes, reeds, scrub and small trees, held a big surprise. Back in the swamp, frogs called harshly. There in the lagoon, like big black peas with tails, thousands of tadpoles wriggled. The last time I saw tadpoles was five years ago, in a tiny shallow backwater on the Tongariro; but there must be tadpoles too in the shallow swamp at the northern end of Whakaipo Bay.

Sitting under a tree for lunch, I contemplated the different shades of blue investing the lake and the hills and the sky to the south. Even the snow on the National Park mountains took on a faint blue tinge. It was that kind of day.

As I watched, one or two fish began to respond to the new presence of green beetles on the water. Thirty metres out, they sipped unhurriedly from the surface, plainly engaged in beetling rather than in smelting. If they had been taking smelt, frantic splashy chases would have betrayed the pursuit of small fish by large fish; but beetles lie fidgeting helplessly on the surface — easy meat.

One or two diminutive wreaths of cloud hovered above the mountains. Otherwise the sky remained an unblemished blue. Typically — and always uncannily — the cloud wreaths continually changed shaped and direction almost as I watched, until I turned my back on them and retraced those tortuous steps to the Mapara Stream.

On the way, two damselflies took tentative wing, newly transformed from underwater creatures into delicate flying insects. I saw two paired adults also, looking at first sight like a single slender-bodied, ruby-red dragonfly. Shining cuckoos and chaffinches called, and the willows bowed and curtsied all along the shore. Close to the stream-mouth, where wind and waves had already covered shoreline rocks with an early carpet of soft green weed, honeybees hummed. Dozens of them busied themselves on the damp green mass. What were they doing there? Were they taking moisture from the weed, or fibres?

Over the way, under the distant cliffs where the boats had been, nothing disturbed the wrinkled blue surface of the sparkling lake. Not quite 24 hours earlier, though, the bay had reeled under sudden lashing squalls of rain and hail borne on a savage blow from the northeast. As I looked out on the smiling face of the lake this day, I wasn't to know that the fury the day before had taken the lives of the two elderly men whose battered dinghy had already been discovered. Their bodies had been retrieved several hours before from 10 metres of water close to the forbidding western shore. Apparently they had been ill-equipped for an emergency, and an emergency had overtaken them. Taupo-Moana, the Sea of Taupo, cannot be trifled with.

Day in the hills

Clear in my mind's eye a gleaming brown trout leaps from the river; at a guess a kilo, maybe a kilo and a half. It curved back into the white water at the head of the pool as gracefully as it left it.

I know its brief essay into my element was no mirage, and yet I couldn't help wondering. So soon after my start with the Claret Nymph at the pool below Bishop's did it rise into view, and as mysteriously vanish again.

Was it trying to tell me something? My day was already enchanted enough, and perhaps the magic of it had cast a spell over me, but here were gathered, on this December morning, all the summer wonders that endear the river to me, and I was caught up in a quiet ecstasy. Was the fish a harbinger of greater joys to come?

Sometimes the river frowns. I have known days of utter misery there, when nothing comes to the fly anywhere, and the rain pelts down, and the parka leaks, and you go home in the evening wet and exhausted, scratched and bruised, and only begin to recover composure after the second large dram.

Misery lurked very low this day. I suppose some fishers would equate misery with lost fish, and I certainly lost fish. I would like to have landed two of those lost ones, especially the second, which went for a special fly Gil gave me, and kept it.

But lost fish are no more a misery to this fisherman than lost trout flies — unless they happen to be Gil's Specials. Even so, my memories of that day evoke only joy. The chuckling river ran clear and pleasantly full. The sun shone from a deep blue and cloudless sky. Early summer growth danced in the breeze all day. Seven fish came willingly to the nymph (though five of them just as willingly let go again). And I was wading wet, in rubber and canvas jungle boots, and stayed warm in the heat of the early summer sun all day.

31

So, already enchanted at the start by the feel of the morning and the look of the first pool tumbling towards me in sparkling sunshine, perhaps a fancy that a leaping fish was trying to tell me something could be excused.

Ten or 20 casts later I hooked that fish. I am sure it was the same one. Surprise shot it out of the water three times, and then the hook came away. I wondered if it was the small brown trout I had caught and returned two years before at the same spot. I also wondered why only one fish appeared to inhabit the pool.

I tried a Green Beetle first, on the off chance that summer was far enough advanced thereabouts to have accustomed fish to the terrestrial. But no beetle flew that day that I could see, and none floated down the river, and I saw no rise to anything all day.

A Claret Nymph deceived that fish, and it deceived a much smaller rainbow in the tail of Bishop's. The tail of Bishop's is at present virtually all that's left of a once hospitable pool from which, before the big flood redistributed many of the river's features a few years ago, good fishermen would take a couple of fish on each occasion they went there.

Thinking back, especially about the Claret Nymph, I know now that I would have hooked more fish if only I had remembered the advice I gave myself years ago and too often forget on the river until it's time to go home: it's the heavy nymph that takes the most fish. This advice was particularly appropriate that day, for the fish lay in the pools, and as the river is quite fast you need to sink the nymph quickly to have it travel the length of the pool low down. Regrettably, the Claret Nymph wasn't really heavy enough.

I forgot something else, too — that the best fish lie in the best positions, and the best positions are usually at the heads of pools, and to fish the heads of pools with a nymph you have to pitch it into the start of the white water well above, so that the current quickly forces it down.

Here and there, besides Bishop's, pools have changed. That's the exciting thing about rivers and streams unspoilt by the hand of man. Even though a heavy cloudburst will sweep familiar runs and pools — and even fish — into oblivion, they'll be back. The more things change, the more they stay the same.

That buttress of rock on the left of the odd little pool where the river comes together again around the corner below the straight running down from Portland's, still stands in 2 metres of water, as of old, and the underwater spit of sand a couple of metres out from it is still only waist deep.

Harry and I crossed the river below the buttress one blazing summer day, and welcomed the cooling sluices of water suddenly pouring over the tops of our thigh boots. Today's level differed only fractionally from that time with Harry; waist deep it was, and briefly breathtaking. But I stood there and fished up, for here was a legacy of the big flood, a splendid new pool. It was tricky to fish because of the willow reaching across from the other bank, and the toetoe behind.

The slim caddis imitation brought a fish to it almost before it had time to sink. The trout must have been lying shallow or else rushed to it from deeper water to beat another fish. He let go almost immediately.

I went on up, searching the deeper pockets in the straight below Portland's, but nothing was home that wanted a nymph. Possibly nothing was home anyway. Pocket water is only home for this river's trout after weeks of hot summer suns. That time lay a long way off.

Buttercups glistened from the banks. Hereabouts, in the hills, summer lagged behind, and with the late yellow buttercups went late yellow broom, late yellow hawkweeds and the unwelcome late yellow of gorse. As a complete contrast, the purple of new foxgloves glowed boldly from a profusion of riverside grasses.

These simple visual joys are food and drink for the soul.

Above the wreck of Portland's a deep new pool lies open to the afternoon sun. This was the pool in which I would christen the first of Gil's identical twins, wet flies tied with special natural fibres which possibly have never before been incorporated into an artificial trout fly. A dark-green and gold caddis went on as a weighted tail fly, Gil's experiment as a dropper.

The third cast brought a sharp response, and a broad silver-white side with a rosy streak somersaulted downstream underwater towards me. The fish may have leapt once, but I don't really remember; I was too interested in establishing which of the two flies it had taken. Only half-concentrating, I switched the landing net from right shoulder to left shoulder. Something snapped. It was the dropper. The fish was free. Gil's fly had proved itself. Sadly, and without much hope, I tied its twin to a new dropper and sent it up the pool. Another fish had it like a tiger, a rainbow of half a kilogram or so, which dashed all over the place. I bustled it into the net. It, too, had taken the dropper.

Gil's remaining masterpiece now sits safely in the small fly box. I won't use it again before, hopefully, its creator can be persuaded to send me a couple more to keep it company.

If the brown trout that leapt at the start of the day had a message for me at all, it was this: Welcome to the river! Welcome to the day!

The river indeed made me welcome, and I had one of the happiest days there I have ever spent.

A *mayflies man*

Angler, amateur entomologist and photographer Bill Crawford aims at capturing on 35mm film the three stages — nymph, dun and spinner — of as many species of New Zealand mayflies as he can find. That's a tall order.

His photographs in the Tichborne Anglers' Calendar for 1993, and others on the April page of the previous year's calendar — including one showing him almost tied in a knot to take a stream insect picture — graphically illustrate some, but only some, of the difficulties and rewards on the way to achieving the Crawford ultimate.

To begin with, Bill really needs a totally shockproof and waterproof camera to vent his frustrations on. You see, he believes the only proper way to photograph hatching nymphs, duns and spinners is while they are very much alive and in their own natural surroundings. He photographs them exactly where and when he finds them, and he uses only the light that falls naturally upon them at the time. Such self-imposed conditions make for excruciating frustrations, as becomes all the more apparent when Bill tells you that, because his volatile subjects are so unpredictable and all too briefly occupy only the most awkward places, using a tripod is quite out of the question. He must therefore anchor the camera, hand-held, against a convenient rock, for the long exposures — sometimes up to a second in length — he needs to secure an adequate depth of focus for his obligatory close-ups.

The frustrations inherent in this natural-photography philosophy are infinite in number and variety. Bill has sampled most of them, several times over. You can't tell him a thing about Murphy's Law, which says that if it is at all possible for things to go wrong, they will.

Take one day in January last, when Bill found an *Oniscigaster wakefieldi* mayfly nymph, a favourite species of his, newly emerged from the water, sitting on a small rock. Maybe here was a chance to capture a hatching sequence? Quickly lining up the camera, but realising he had only six frames left on the film, Bill prepared to take his first picture. At this point the sun clouded over. Murphy was on his way. The nymph was beginning to hatch, so one picture had to be taken in the dull light. The sun reappeared. Bill quickly took two more photographs as the mayfly emerged through the split thorax of its nymphal shuck.

Murphy suddenly arrived. He quickly sized up the situation and gleefully went to work. Bill's left side and arm were already immersed in the stream, and his left hand, holding the camera, was partly submerged. Many of Bill's photographs are taken in just such a situation simply because, unlike damselfly or dragonfly nymphs for instance, the nymphs of mayfly species which crawl out of the water to hatch normally come to a stop only just above water level.

Murphy whistled up some gusts of wind. These raised a chop on the river and threw spray around. Bill had to scramble away from water level to avoid sudden waves washing over the camera. The same waves temporarily dislodged the nymph. As soon as the wind dropped, Bill sprawled on the stones again and managed to get another shot of the emerging mayfly before it cleared the shuck. That was four frames gone. The next picture was a failure because Murphy nudged the camera just as Bill released the shutter on the newly emerged dun. The insect had already turned to face upwind, and now it shuffled into a new position. Bill had to line up the camera yet again, and use his left eye instead of his right after easing himself into a most uncomfortable new position in the river. The shutter clicked on the last picture. It was all over.

In spite of Murphy's close interest on that occasion, and apart from the first and fifth frames, the sequence turned out well. The other four photographs were all perfectly focused and exposed. Success on such occasions is very sweet, and more than makes up for all the short-fuse frustrations Bill meets along the way.

A quite different frustration has plagued him ever since his delight in trout-fishing opened up a side interest, trout-stream entomology, 10 years ago: lack of definitive information about some New Zealand mayflies.

Many of the 30-odd species of New Zealand mayflies which have so far been "officially" identified and described cannot be confused one with the other. Most serious fly-fishers are familiar with the more distinctive ones, either in nymph, dun or spinner forms: for instance, the widely distributed spiny-gilled mayfly *Coloburiscus humeralis*; our big and much less common mayfly *Ichthybotus hudsoni*; the gregarious swimming mayfly *Oniscigaster wakefieldi*; the reddish-orange, double-gilled *Acanthophlebia cruentata*.

However, no single key to all three stages — nymph, dun and spinner — of all the New Zealand mayflies exists. No scientist is working continuously on these insects. While the economy is in the shape it is, Bill cannot see any definitive study being conducted, unless at the instigation of some fly-fishing philanthropist prepared to fund such a study for at least the few years it would take to research and solve the mayflies puzzle. Until or unless that happens, anglers and entomologists will have to make do with incomplete information.

Bill is particularly anxious to see all *Deleatidium* species properly identified and described. This big genus concerns him so much that, once he has found and photographed as many mayflies as he can of all the other New Zealand genera, he will concentrate purely on the genus *Deleatidium*.

When that time comes, both his insect photographs and the slides he makes of mayfly wings may well help to identify more species. Don't be in the least surprised if, some day in the future, an entirely new species of *Deleatidium* emerges and is named *Deleatidium crawfordi* in honour of its discoverer.

Lack of professional research is disappointing enough without the mistakes and misunderstandings it generates among keen trout-fishers and fly-tiers. For instance, the origins of one of New Zealand's most famous artificials, the Kakahi Queen, have been sourced to at least two quite different species. Highly respected anglers differ substantially on the identity of the fly on which an early Kakahi postmaster, Basil Humphrey, is presumed by some to have based the pattern. It was tied as a dry fly, but the body colour of the artificial dun differs considerably from the body colour of either of the duns of the nominated naturals, *Ameletopsis perscitus* and *Coloburiscus humeralis*. Bill is now sure that the Kakahi Queen dry-fly pattern was not based on either of these species at all, but on one of the *Nesameletus* species still common in the Whakapapa around Kakahi (species which, admittedly, are postulated by at least one authority as Mr Humphrey's alternative model).

Until a year or so ago, Bill took all his photographs on an old Praktica MTL 3 35mm camera with a Zeiss Tessar 2.8 50mm lens and one, two or sometimes three extension tubes. Now he uses a Nikon 601 35mm camera with motor drive and a Nikkor 60mm micro lens. Formerly, most of his insect and scenic photographs were taken on Kodachrome ISO 64 slide film. Now, as well as Kodachrome 64, which he finds more faithfully reproduces natural colours than other slide films, he uses a standard ISO 400 print film. Like all photographers, he likes to see the results of his endeavours as soon as possible, hence his increasing use of print film; also, of course, the fastish film speed of ISO 400 allows him shorter exposures without loss of depth of field — a vital consideration where close-up, live-insect photography is concerned. The 2–3mm gained in depth of field can make all the difference between a pleasingly sharp image and a disappointingly fuzzy one.

Like so many photographers of wildlife, Bill Crawford has come to admire his particular subjects. He has a special regard for nymphs of the genus *Oniscigaster*, those gregarious, flattened swimmers which sometimes flit away from the shallow-wading fly-fisher like a shoal of mini-flounders. In fact, having taken one 45km to his home one day to examine under the microscope, Bill returned it to the place it had come from on his next photography trip.

Nymphs living on the undersides of rocks cannot normally be photographed in their natural surroundings. Bill borrows them from the river, photographs them in a collector's net, bottle or dish, and then returns them.

What fish he catches these days are all caught and released too. Once upon a time he was as keen a fly-fisher as the next man, but close study of trout and their food, and thorough exploration of scores of miles of central North Island rivers and streams, spotting fish and insects, have turned him into more of a fly-catcher with camera than a fish-catcher with artificial fly. So often he carries a rod, all set up to catch fish, only in order to persuade the curious onlooker that he's just another eccentric fisherman poking about, rather than an amateur entomologist–photographer looking for mayflies.

All the same, Bill Crawford is an exceptional fly-fisher. If the mood takes him — as it did only a week or so ago, on a grudgingly sunny day, with the hillsides around all white with manuka blossom, and the pair of us celebrating the New Year in advance, in the time-honoured way — trout had better look out.

Bill was apparently favouring a large Royal Wulff; but he had only tied it on because, if he decided to fish at all that day, he considered it most unlikely that any self-respecting brown trout would fall victim to it. He was wrong. Two biggish fish went for it. The first, which would have been closer to 3kg than 2kg, hardly knew what had happened before it was back in the river: Bill plays, lands and releases his fish faster than anyone I know. The second, unhappily, broke him on a strong downstream rush. Bill cursed, not for the loss of his Royal Wulff, but for leaving the fly in the fish. He said he ought to have retied the fly after landing the first fish. And so he should.

Yet nobody's perfect. Even this angler–entomologist perfectionist doesn't fish perfectly all the time, which is a relief to habitual bunglers like me. But he would dearly like some specialist in aquatic entomology to complete the identification and description of all New Zealand mayfly species; and the sooner the better.

He quips, grinning, in his Belfast brogue: "Entomology in New Zealand? It's a can of worms!"

Summer

New Year's Day

Yesterday, New Year's Day, I beat the system. Often and often the system decrees that the day I select to go fishing shall bare its teeth at me.

It shall rain heavily. Only a miserable 12cm trout shall come to hand, and the hand shall be unable to unhook the fish until the thing is at its last gasp, barely returnable.

I shall forget to take lunch, or a spare line. I shall lose a precious box of flies, and the flies I am left with shall develop a touching affection for toetoe and treetops, to which they shall cling immovably.

Yesterday, however, the snagged flies came free. I didn't once have to break one off. I started out at the Apple Orchard with a weighted Hare and Copper nymph, and I finished up hours later with the same fly safe and sound.

No, that's not quite true. It was certainly the same fly, but a somewhat sorrier specimen than the one with which I had begun. Ten trout progressively mauled it, nine rainbows and a brown, until almost as much bare copper wire as hare fur showed.

I remembered to take lunch, and I remembered to buy a pack of fruit juice to go with it. I did forget a sinking line, but it was a deliberate lapse, because I knew I would be fishing a floating line upstream the whole time, and moreover the kind of fishing country I would be moving through demanded that I should travel light, unencumbered except for an essential minimum of gear in the day pack.

As for the weather — well, you may remember that the day before yesterday, New Year's Eve, blew itself inside out. White horses galloped madly north up the lake to Taupo town. Trees waved frantically all day.

At sunset, parties of gulls, 10 or more of them at a time, beat slowly south, tossed this way and that, but always forging ahead in the comparative shelter below the high ridges above Acacia Bay. Then they would rise up, dim, white, energetic bits of flotsam tossed about against the backlit gloom of pine trees, and disappear over the skyline treetops into the sunset glare.

I seem to have witnessed similar migrations south, on fiercely windy evenings at this time of year, before. No doubt the gulls were finding the lake-shore at Taupo untenable, but why didn't they shelter in Acacia Bay rather than fight their way further south? Were they heading for nesting sites on the sheltered faces of the Western Bay cliffs? Surely, though, they don't leave their mating and nesting time until the end of December?

Mercifully, late that evening, the gale blew itself out. At midnight the moon rode in a clear, quiet sky, and the sound of bagpipes and revellers' cheers carried far into the still air of the new year.

Morning broke utterly calm. No cloud cluttered the sky. This would be a day for fishing the Waipunga: and so it proved, a glorious day, all sunshine and faint breezes, and lush green growth everywhere, and daisies and foxgloves standing tall, and the pig fern only just unfolding the arms that love to trap the fly-line and the meshes of the landing net.

I almost left the net in the car at the Apple Orchard, knowing that a thousand grasping green and brown hands lay in wait for it along the way. Common sense prevailed. I am a catch-and-release man, and the Waipunga is a catch-and-release river. You can't catch and safely release fish unless you observe three rules: first, you must use barbless hooks; second, you must use at least a 3kg breaking-strain tippet; and third, you must land fish in a landing net. These three rules ensure that hooks are quickly removed, and fish landed and released quickly and without damage. The longer you play a fish, the more exhausted it becomes and the less likely it is to survive the encounter; so you bundle it into the net as fast as you can, still in the water, turn and face downstream, jam the rod between your legs, gently grasp the fish in the folds of the net at the surface, turn the fish on its back and remove the hook, and then send your temporary captive on its way rejoicing.

I did that yesterday six or seven times. The other three or four fish I hooked came unstuck almost as soon as I felt them. Barbless hooks teach you to keep the line taut from start to finish, and I am still learning, although I don't lose as many now as I used to.

Not surprisingly, nothing came to the Hare and Copper fly in the Apple Orchard Pool itself, the pool to which the narrow track from the highway leads you. Judging by the freedom with which the angler can navigate the track at present, through an area overgrown with scrub and blackberry, one or two fishermen regularly thread their way along it to fish the Apple Orchard Pool, even if they don't venture far beyond it.

Yesterday, having drawn a blank there, I refused to accept the corollary that the next pool up, and the next, would be similarly devoid of fish. My optimism was rewarded. I was especially pleased that the next pool held fish, for if ever a pool promised sport, this is it; and yet in the past it has always disappointed. Yesterday it smiled, to the extent of

41

three fish hooked and one of them landed.

After that, fish came here and there from likely places, some from deep pools and some from rollicking riffles. The heaviest fish would have weighed 1.5kg, a dour, red-striped rainbow jack from the deepest pool. Pool fish rarely react spectacularly; it's the 1kg and 1.5kg trout from behind the rocks in the riffles that, feeling the hook, dash around demented, bursting out of the water time and again in horror-struck surprise.

One place, and only one, intimidates the angler who wants to fish up beyond a rushing narrowing of the river along the Apple Orchard stretch. Sheer rock faces and steep banks clad in virtually impenetrable scrub tend to encourage the fisherman to stick to the water and work his way along the buttress of rock on the right-hand side, wading almost waist deep in a heavy flow. Last time there, Bill led the way. I inched up the rush of water in his slipstream, so to speak, but yesterday I was on my own, and I couldn't battle up further than halfway. If only the rock face sloped away from the river at that point I might have fought my way to the head of the chute, but it almost leans out over you, and offers no secure handholds.

I backed off, climbed up into the thick scrub and old pig fern, and found a way back to the river upstream of the rapids through the dense manuka along the hillside.

Those are the times when landing nets and other external impedimenta take a fiendish delight in clutching everything within reach. Of course, some folding nets come in sheaths which keep the meshes out of the way, but my net is a big one with a round mouth and is not collapsible. I can either gather up the folds of it in my left hand and steer the net free of trouble — but this means that, with the rod in my right hand, I have no free hand to part bushes and free the line every so often — or I can hang the net on its elasticised cord directly down my back, underneath the pack.

All in all, yesterday was nonetheless a rewarding, if tiring, fishing day. I even remembered the way out of the river by way of a little gully, which this year isn't as seriously complicated by blackberry as I first thought. Once on the highway, with holidaymakers' fast cars rushing to or from Taupo, I walked back to my own vehicle in 15 minutes.

Today, the day after New Year's Day, cloud fills the sky, the occasional shower of rain infinitesimally relieves our parched farmland, forests and gardens, and a nagging wind corrugates the lake and grapples with the trees again. It is a day not too unlike the roaring unpleasantness of New Year's Eve. How lucky we were with the New Year's Day sandwiched between!

Home-delivered fly-tying feathers

In four days a greenfinch, a waxeye and a blackbird have died on the cobblestones alongside the house. Almost certainly they flew into the glass of an upstairs window and broke their necks. Fortunately, such accidents don't usually occur more than a couple of times a year, but when they do, the feathers are welcome.

Saturday's greenfinch was a hen. I tweaked numbers of small soft feathers from breast, rump and wing coverts.

Monday's waxeye disappeared before Margaret could tell me of the casualty lying on the cobblestones. I would have felt the loss of dozens of soft grey and green and rusty-brown feathers more keenly had I not already helped myself to a collection from the waxeye that suffered a similar fate a year ago.

Tuesday's fatality brought a treasure-trove of beautiful small feathers. The blackbird was a comparative youngster, clad in speckled brown feathers well suited to the imitation of many of our stream flies, whether as nymphs, pupae, duns or spinners.

Nothing imparts the appearance of life to small nymphs and wet flies so well as the soft fibres of small-bird feathers. The more speckled they are, the more successful they are likely to be. Plain, all-over colour in feathers for bodies and legs is better avoided in favour of variegated feathers.

So long as it doesn't repel because it is totally unnatural, a meal virtually sparkling with interest will appeal more than a plain one. I don't know about your palate, but mine responds to exciting-looking food as positively as the trout's palate. Hence the importance of speckled and multi-toned feathers and fibres, blended furs, discreet gold tags, and gold or silver ribbing.

Plain patterns won't catch and reflect light. Within reason, the more an artificial does catch the light, especially in medium to fast rivers and streams, the faster the trout will see it. The faster they see it, the more likely they are to intercept it and gratefully inhale it.

My so recently acquired collection of small speckled feathers will, I hope, end up in irresistibly variegated imitations. But when I'm tying, I must remember two guiding principles for small nymphs and wet flies: the bodies of the naturals are slim; and they have only six legs. If you aim at deceiving trout with patterns imitating, or caricaturing, some aquatic insect or other, tie the bodies slim and keep the leg hackles sparse. Artificials tied that way look more natural and provoke little suspicion. Thick bunches of fibres inhibit the appearance of life that fewer fibres give. No matter that just a few legs, moving seductively around, will not survive many encounters with trout: you just have to carry sufficient replacement flies around.

W.C. Stewart, the great Scots exponent of the upstream wet fly, loved his soft-hackled "spiders". He warned anglers not to tie them too bushy. Even so, with too much hackle the flies would still prove irresistible; and anyway, after a dozen trout had tackled one of his spiders, Stewart said, the hackle would become "spare enough".

Twelve of the best

Fishing books are numbered in their thousands, but classic fishing books are few and far between.

When an angler achieves a confidence in his fishing which takes him beyond the realms of the manuals telling him what to do and where to go, he can, if he wants to take his reading further, step into a wonderful world of angling literature — a world which, incidentally, he can never hope to explore completely. There are just too many books.

Angling has the most, and the most literate, and the most lyrical, writers of any sport. I receive a few second-hand fishing book catalogues every year. Two of them together always list more than 2,000 books. That's not to say that all of them are first class, but the consistently large number of angling books forever changing hands indicates just how immense the demand for them is, and how immense is the literature itself. It is far larger than that of any other sport. By comparison, rugby and cricket together offer only a token literature.

The world of angling books has introduced me to all kinds of angling experience, theory, philosophy and reminiscence. Among the mass of often distinguished and always, for me, enjoyable volumes, certain books stand out triumphantly from the rest.

Others may not share my enthusiasm for the special dozen books I favour; but I think that when — not if — trout-fishers turn from the strictly practical fishing handbooks to more relaxed reading, these 12 books will introduce them as well as any to the kind of pleasures awaiting anglers ready to explore the many-splendoured world of fishing literature.

By and large, my 12 are mainly about fishing, but one of the English ones and one of the American ones stray into associated matters — such as wildfowling, old and new trout flies, wildlife and famous fly-fishers.

I chose this dozen for the pleasure the books have given me and continue to give me. Some, in passing, do teach useful things, but chiefly you learn of the authors' delight in fishing and fishing's companion pleasures. For me, the writers' happy, literate, thoughtful and often scholarly ways with angling words and ideas make this selection especially memorable.

Some of the books are available from one or other of our public libraries. If the local library does not itself have copies, it's likely that another library will. If so, an inter-loan request will secure them.

As for the other books — well, they may be out of print, which means they can only be bought, if you're lucky, from a second-hand bookshop. If they can't be borrowed from a friend, they may one day turn up in a catalogue issued by a seller of second-hand fishing books.

My dozen is made up of four books set in England, four books set mainly in North America and four set in New Zealand. They cover all sorts of appealing angling-related interests: coarse fishing on the River Thames, trout-fishing in Brittany, fly-fishing innovations, wildfowling, love affairs with classic cars, tracking down the grave of a famous American fly-fisher, a scholarly miscellany of fly-fishing history, old books, a mixture of sporting days in England and Canada, and delightful angling and other reminiscences of New Zealand mixed in with a few of Australia.

First there is Chalmers, Patrick Chalmers. He wrote a wonderful book called *At the Tail of the Weir*. It's all about the fishing of the River Thames. His writing is a bit precious, his effects a little contrived, but that's just his way with words, which is otherwise delightful, easy, anecdotal, discursive, often how-to-do-it but never textbookishly so. Nostalgia looms large in the enjoyment of angling books, and Chalmers generates that sort of enjoyment. Whether or not you have ever fished in England is immaterial.

That book was published in 1932. The next one is older, Romilly Fedden's *Golden Days*, published in 1919. It is subtitled *From the Fishing Log of a Painter in Brittany*. The author wrote much of it in 1918 close to the mud and blood and stench of death in France towards the end of the First World War. I particularly like his account of the "hatch" of mayflies engineered by Jean Pierre and his daughter.

My next one is even older. This is a book by that incredible Englishman Mottram, whose ideas were far in advance of his time. The only thing I hold against this man is that he later sided with those chalk-stream

When the trout are on the move up the Waitahanui, De Lautour's Pool sprouts anglers.
These three hopefuls standing at the junction with the Mangamutu Stream are fishing lures
downstream into the body of this famous pool, which lies directly upstream of the bridge over
State Highway 1.

Snow may still lie deep on the Tongariro National Park mountains, but when the broom froths yellow at Whakaipo, you know it's spring.

This is a small nematomorph, or hairworm, of 40 mm or so, found on the banks of the Tongariro. Others, swallowed by trout subsequently caught by the author, were 10 times as long.

Some say Sam Parsons' Parsons' Glory (left) is a Dorothy, but Sam was the son of the famous fly's inventor, Phil Parsons, and he really ought to have known what fly he was tying. The other fly is a present-day version of the original Parsons' Glory.

If you fancy yourself as a nature photographer, try finding and expertly photographing in situ a small Nesameletus mayfly subimago like this one, just emerged from its nymphal shuck. And the best of luck! (Photo: Bill Crawford)

Depending on the density of your sinking line, you allow between one and two minutes for the lure to reach bottom at Whakamoenga, and then you begin a slow retrieve.

This may be his day for the big one, for he's fishing at Lake Otamangakau, the North Island's trophy trout water.

bigots who virtually blacklisted poor Skues and ended the old man's 56-year-old love affair with the River Itchen because they wouldn't let him nymph-fish there any longer.

So much of interest to fly-fishers is tucked away in Mottram's book, which he called *Fly Fishing: Some New Arts and Mysteries* and which was published in 1914. I particularly like the accounts of his New Zealand experiences in 1911 or so, and his imaginative last chapter, on catch and release 100 years in the future.

If you have watched the *Survival* series of natural history programmes on television you will know the name Colin Willock, the writer and producer of so many of them. He wrote a book called *Landscape with Solitary Figure*. It's about his fishing, his duck-shooting in the heart of London, his love of an Alvis sports car, his experiences with some famous English anglers, and the legendary wildfowler and poacher of the Fens, Kenzie Thorpe.

Over the past 30 years or so, North Americans have written so much more of value on angling than the British; but having said that, it was a former Englishman who wrote, from his home in Canada, one of the finest fishing books I have ever read. He was Roderick Haig-Brown, and his book was *A River Never Sleeps*. It presents Canadian and English fishing and associated pleasures and reminiscences in fascinating array.

The second of my North Americans is a book called *Quill Gordon*, by John McDonald, who was an exceptionally gifted fly-fisher, writer and scholar. The book ranges over the origins of angling, Theodore Gordon (the legendary American fly-fisher), hallowed American waters, old and new flies, Dame Juliana Berners and her *Treatise*, and so on.

Alfred W. Miller, under the pen name Sparse Grey Hackle, wrote the third of my American selection, *Fishless Days, Angling Nights*. Like John McDonald, he enjoyed researching and writing about a whole host of interests outside the mere catching of fish, often very humorously.

John Volker also wrote humorously and under a pseudonym. He called himself Robert Traver. He wrote that outstandingly successful novel *Anatomy of a Murder*. He also wrote a fishing book called *Anatomy of a Fisherman*, but fishing doesn't command the attention murder does, and anyway it is mainly a book of photographs, with commentary and captions by Traver, and it didn't enjoy the success of the novel. One of his other books, however — *Trout Madness* — almost did. This is an often very amusing series of his fishing adventures, largely in search of brook trout, all set in Michigan, where Volker was a district attorney.

This is the man who once wrote that fly-fishing was the most pleasurable thing a man could do standing up . . . But he also wrote a personal testament of fishing, which goes like this:

> I fish because I love to; because I love the environs where trout are found, which are invariably beautiful, and hate the environs where crowds of people are found, which are invariably ugly; because of all the television commercials, cocktail parties, and associated social posturing I thus escape; because, in a world where most men seem to spend their lives doing things they hate, my fishing is at once an endless source of delight and an act of small rebellion; because trout do not lie or cheat and cannot be bought or bribed or impressed by power, but respond only to quietude and humility and endless patience; because I suspect that men are going along this way for the last time, and I for one don't want to waste the trip; because mercifully there are no telephones on trout waters; because only in the woods can I find solitude without loneliness; because bourbon out of an old tin cup always tastes better out there; because maybe one day I will catch a mermaid; and, finally, not because I regard fishing as being so terribly important but because I suspect that so many of the other concerns of men are equally unimportant — and not nearly so much fun.

This cry from the heart of John Volker did not come from *Trout Madness* but from his *Anatomy of a Fisherman*.

Trout Madness has a subtitle: *Being a Dissertation on the Symptoms and Pathology of this Incurable Disease by One of its Victims*; which at once prepares the reader for what is to come.

The first book of my New Zealand quartet is O.S. Hintz's *Trout at Taupo*. Trout-fishers are not always enamoured of Taupo trout-fishing, but this one is a classic, and in Hintz's day his beloved Waitahanui River and many of the players on his Taupo stage were classics too. Hintz may not have been able to see far past his big-lure, downstream fishing for rainbows in the rip or up the river, but he wrote superbly of it: he was, after all, a first-class journalist. When he wrote his book he was associate editor of New Zealand's great newspaper, the *New Zealand Herald*.

Derisley Hobbs, a one-time New Zealand Marine Department freshwater fisheries authority, had an architect brother equally keen on trout-fishing, G.B. Hobbs, who lived most of his life in England but who came back occasionally to New Zealand to fish. In the same year, 1955, that Budge Hintz published his book, G.B. Hobbs published his *Fisherman's Country*, one of the few worthwhile mixtures of fly-fishing travel, personal experience and advice produced in New Zealand so far.

Greg Kelly's is another of the worthwhile mixtures. Maybe because I knew Greg I am especially fond of his book *The Flies in My Hat*, an absorbing collection of fishing memories of many waters in both islands. Greg was 97 when he died in Taupo. Many will know that he was a hunter in earlier years, and wrote a hunting book, *Gun in the Hills*. His other book of guns, *The Gun in the Case*, was a series of investigations into murders and other police cases involving guns, for he was for many years the Police Department's ballistics expert. I own all three books (and the little instructional book on trout-fishing he also wrote), but the one I come back to time and time again is *The Flies in My Hat*.

Douglas Stewart is the author of my twelfth and last book. His *The Seven Rivers* tells of his fishing in Taranaki and, later, in Australia, where he became so celebrated a writer and poet that the Australians gladly adopted him as one of their own.

Stewart spent most of his life in Australia, just as Greg Kelly, originally an Australian, spent most of his in New Zealand. As one would expect of a man who gained journalistic skills on three Taranaki newspapers, and who later became the literary editor of the *Sydney Bulletin*, he wrote of his fishing days, and the people of his fishing adventures, with the enviable skill of the true professional.

These are only 12 of the best. How lucky we are that there are many more dozens of worthy books among the thousands with which angling is blessed!

Good luck, Fred!

Down by the water, along the sheltered mudstone shore of Lake Otamangakau's McGivern's Bay, dozens of dainty damselflies fluttered. Back in the scrub up the bank, scores of cicadas chased about. If you walked through the crowded manuka, ling heather and old dry broom branches up there, cicadas would scatter everywhere, thudding against your hat, blundering into spiders' webs, rocketing into the stiff breeze of morning.

Unhappily, that same stiff breeze of morning dashed cicada after cicada to the surface of the lake. Those flung into the calm water close to the McGivern's Bay shore wriggled and spun, wriggled and spun. Some were pale green, some pale brown, and some dark brown. One took off again from the water, the only one I saw escape.

All the others drifted away before the wind into the waves driving north-east, some into the hungry mouths of cruising trout. Sometimes the trout sent spray flying with the enthusiasm of their strikes; sometimes they merely golloped noisily at the surface. It was as though the big insects intimidated the fish, which didn't quite know what to make of them. They could have sipped them quietly down without any risk of losing them, for the insects weren't going to escape. Instead, the fish chose to lash out at them.

A few days before, Brian had said the fish were slapping the cicadas with their tails. Today, it appeared that they were doing the same again.

Most of the insects finished up not in trout at all but in black swans. True, mallard and seagulls took their share, but the 50 or 60 swans I watched patrolling alertly up and down the lake took most. Usually, swans feeding on Lake Otamangakau show you their nether regions much of the time. The lake is shallow in many places, and the birds tip up to graze the weeds below.

Today, every black swan, old and young, hunted intently for floating cicadas. Normally, the birds don't look around for food; if they are over deep water they merely paddle the few yards to shallow water and reach down for their next snack. What a difference today! None of them sought weed under water; they were all constantly on the lookout for floating cicadas. McGivern's Bay, as it so often does, offered a lee shore. Though cicadas splashed down one after the other, from the bank above, no trout rose to them there in the shallows.

Three hundred metres out, and further, where fly-fishers in five anchored boats sought to bring trout to imitation cicadas, you would suppose that great slaughter was being done. Not so. Once, I think, one angler hooked and lost a fish, and that was all. But the fish continued to come to the real thing: every so often the spray would fly out there as yet another trout made its sudden presence (and a cicada's sudden absence) known.

While I fished, sending wind-assisted casts puny distances towards the boats, a small, shrill band of bickering pied stilts (they are almost as strident as spur-winged plover) wheeled round and round. Did they have young in the scrub?

No fish came to the cicada I flung out time and time again, and at last it was lunch time. I waded gingerly ashore over the slippery mudstone margins to the shady corner where I'd left the day pack.

Five damselfly nymphs clung to the wet meshes of the landing net. Six more clung to the pack, all in various stages of their metamorphosis. I studied the mudstone beach closely, and shook my head in wonder at the quite extraordinary numbers of damselfly nymphs and newly hatched adults littering both sunny and shady sections of the shore.

No wonder the summer fish of Lake Otamangakau grow fat! The proliferation of cicadas and damselflies is beyond calculation. And yet, while on other occasions I have marvelled at the number of adult damselflies on the water — fly-fishers are all too familiar with the phenomenon of the floating fly-line strewn with clinging damselflies — they were today conspicuous by their absence from the water. Perhaps the wind was too strong to encourage them into flight.

Sitting there in the shade, looking out from diminutive McGivern's Bay over the blue waves and anchored boats to the great mass of Mt Tongariro, and beyond that to the snow-streaked crags of Mt Ruapehu, I thought of the man for whom the bay was named. I didn't know it then, but Fred himself would fish his bay the next day with two friends, Bill and Nick, perhaps for the last time. They called it McGivern's because of the frequency, and the success and pleasure, with which Fred fished it 10 to 15

years ago. In those happier days, when Fred fished and guided, and meticulously made and mended rods, Taupo fulfilled all the promise the place had held out to him, first in England and then in Australia. A Lancastrian, Fred finally arrived in Taupo as joyfully as anyone who attains his Shangrila. He loved his fishing, couldn't understand the folk who measured their angling enjoyment only in fish killed, went out of his way to advise on the local fishing, the worth of tackle and books, and continued to devote a rare talent to the careful making and repair of fishing rods.

There came a time, though, when things did not go well for Fred. He drew less and less often on his inexhaustible repertoire of funny stories. Australia called more insistently than in the past: his brothers and his own three grown-up children were there. Small wonder then that Fred and his wife should make the decision to join his folk across the Tasman.

I was to say goodbye to him a few days hence. Meanwhile, today, a photograph or two of McGivern's Bay would need to be taken. One of them would be printed and framed urgently for presentation to him by another of the many Taupo friends of his saddened by his imminent departure.

I continued to have McGivern's Bay to myself after lunch (a circumstance unfortunately as true of fish as of fishermen), but that day I wanted also to explore the shoreline edging some of the big backwater west of the outlet canal, so I was soon on my way there.

Five cars parked in the scrub in the Suez Canal area threatened an over-abundance of fishermen, but in fact only a couple of anchored boats, each manned by one angler, disturbed my solitude; and only one of those boats offended. You know how aluminium boats proclaim their presence? Magnify the slightest sound? Well, the angler in the aluminium dinghy might have been stone-deaf for all he cared for keeping quiet. I imagined fish departing in terror from the clanking metallic rattle of the anchor chain, the dull metallic crash of oars, the echoing metallic sounds of dropped fishing gear. The man appeared to cast competently enough, but didn't he know the age-old fishing dictum, "Study to be quiet"?

The other man cast and cast and cast from an anchored rubber boat. Never a sound came from that quarter; but, like his noisy neighbour, the man caught no fish.

Trout continued to rise intermittently in the shallow chop driving into the big bay. I felt good, content and comfortable. Mind you, the afternoon sun would have been unbearably hot but for the brisk southwesterly breeze.

Cicadas still rose from the scrub and toppled into the water, and though no trout splashed at my imitation for a long time I still felt good about Lake Otamangakau that day. Too often, hours of inactivity there tend to crush the spirit and send the angler home depressed. Believe me, I know. Today was different. The whole place sang.

At length, casting a big green Hussey Cicada into the waves parading past, I jumped in surprise as a fish grabbed a real cicada close to mine. But it *was* mine, and I struck, and the fish was there, and it stayed on, and in three or four minutes I was sliding it over the rim of the landing net — a small, fat rainbow of a kilo or so. I released it, and two casts later a new Hussey Cicada brought a great smashing rise from another fish. I missed that one, dammit.

Cicadas were still flying when I left at half past four. They had been feeding the trout, swans, mallard and gulls for at least five hours of that brilliant, breezy summer's day at Otamangakau.

Day of the cockabullies

Mottled brown cockabullies the size of my little finger lingered down below, quite unafraid. I did not at all like the implication that because they showed no fear there was nothing to fear thereabouts, especially trout.

Normally, they would scurry for their lives at the slightest movement of wadered legs. Today, six of them befriended my presence. One even worked its way slowly up my left wader, resting trustingly every so often. I dropped the Mallard Smelt fly among the little fish a metre below me and jigged it slowly up to the surface. Two cockabullies doggedly attacked it, as if to make up for the absence of trout. I could feel their tiny bites.

I have never before seen so many cockabullies at Whakaipo. True, I have often come away from the bay wondering whether any trout inhabit that place, but today it seemed especially bereft: no trout plucked tentatively at the Mallard Smelt; no trout broke the largely smooth surface of the bay all afternoon.

Away in the Sunday distance, children cried happily from the sandy beach and splashed in the shallows. Five herons flew here, there and everywhere. Fleets of floating thistle-seeds rocked gently close to the shore, and slim paired damselflies pottered gently about over the wet and weedy foreshore. It was strange, but the shore was really wet for some distance above the waterline, and the drying green weed on rocks now standing

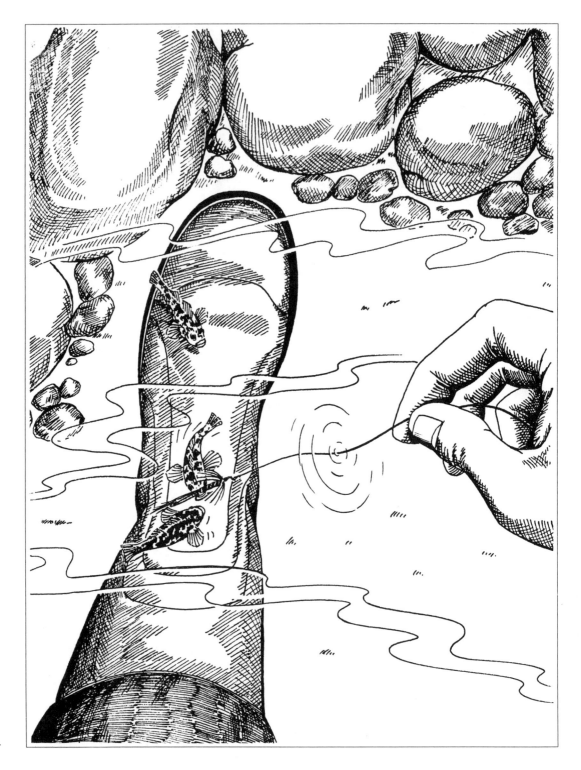

above the surface had surely not been long exposed to the air? The lake must have been dropping fast, and it might not be long before the unsightly smelly beaches of some months ago return.

At times a faint breeze blew, sending diminutive ripples across the bay, but ripples never big enough to excite any interest in trout which might have been lurking out there. Too many still days of sunshine and excessive heat had surely driven the fish into the comfort of deep water. Only with the coming of darkness and a respite from bright light and warm water would some fish venture into the shallows, notably where the Mapara Stream brings cooler water into the bay.

An hour of casting the smelt fly futilely into Gillett's Bay under the burning sun convinced me that it was time for a cup of tea and a rest in the shade. While I dozed, a welcome breeze waxed, and then waned, waxed and waned.

When the lake comes alive under a steady breeze, success looms large, even though you might not quite manage to grasp it every time. A flat calm, by contrast, unless at night, chops confidence very small, so that today, when I made a fresh start, confidence had oozed almost entirely away; the lake lay practically smooth again, and nothing came to the lure except an occasional streamer of weed. I didn't even get a strike from a cockabully.

Cover up!

Summer fly-fishers wading in T-shirts, shorts, sneakers and no hat, need their heads read. For one thing they don't need their heads red, but they get them red all right, and they get red arms and red legs and everything else red that's left uncovered.

Sun block, even the most efficient brand, is only a partial answer, for it gets washed off trout-fishers wading wet, especially those working their way upstream.

Running water will wash blood off scratched and bitten flesh, of course, but you can save the costs of sun block, sunburn, insect repellent, and scratched and sandfly-bitten flesh, by covering up. We'll come to the sneakers later, but clothing for sensible, comfortable wet wading on hot days should comprise tough but lightweight polyester–cotton trousers, long-sleeved shirt, and hat, preferably all green. They may not fit the young male angler's macho image of himself as intrepid angling adventurer, but they sure ward off branches, blackberry and rock edges, and if you fish in the sort of fast summer waters that give the greatest pleasure, a long day free from scratches, bites and sunburn makes the occasion all the more enjoyable.

Wet skin certainly dries faster than wet polyester–cotton, but you wouldn't be wading wet unless the weather was warm anyway, and polyester–cottons quickly dry out.

Naturally, a hat is indispensable now. Some trout-fishers favour a peaked cap, some a soft cotton affair, others a stiffish broad-brimmed hat. The peaked cap may be fashionable right now, but it only shades the eyes. Soft hats with normal-width brims, though obviously floppy, shade the head all round. To my mind, their other outstanding advantages are easy portability off the head, their readiness to conform under a parka hood in the event of rain, and water-retaining capacity. The greatest of these advantages is the latter; nothing is more refreshing on a really hot day than a hat soaked in the stream and put straight back on the head. Stiffish hats

with good broad brims keep the sun off well, but they don't hold cooling water the way soft hats do.

Summer encourages accelerated algal growth on underwater rocks and stones. Footholds secure enough in cooler weather often become dangerously uncertain after weeks of hot summer suns and falling water levels. Even with a companion, wading should be done more circumspectly, not necessarily to avoid the clash of stone on stone (although that should always be a prime consideration), but to reduce the risk of sprains, at worst breaks, especially if you are way out in the sticks somewhere. On your own, the greater the distance you are from help, the greater the care you need to exercise, not just for yourself, but for the sake of the individuals who may have to turn out and find you and get you to a doctor.

Non-slip wading boots are obligatory. Even if the old styles perform well — and cleats, studs, wading "irons" and deep tread do perform well — the only surface worth considering for wading of all kinds is felt or carpet bonded to soles and heels. However carefully you seem to wade, metal plates or studs eventually send out warning sounds. But unless you accidentally kick one stone against another, felt or carpet soles keep you quiet; and after sneakers or other footwear, the assurance felt soles give is uncanny.

If you can afford it, buy the best felt soles from a tackle shop, and ask to have them bonded to your boots. Alternatively, cut soles from top-quality wool or nylon carpet, cut the tread off your boots, and bond the soles (and separate heels) to the smooth surfaces with a waterproof contact glue.

Some anglers favour substantial, often heavy, boots for summer wading, but the rubber-soled type with green canvas uppers reaching 15cm or so up the calf may be worn all day without the least fatigue.

Tribute to Greg

George was painting round the back somewhere. When the bell jangled he had to put down his brush and pot of paint, come cursing silently down the ladder, and then appear cheerfully to whoever it was in the shop.

"George! Just a block of chocolate and three Royal Wulffs," I said, "then you can get back to your painting."

He grinned. I told him I was taking the day off, heading into Greg Kelly country around Kakahi on the Whakapapa, quite some way off. Then I got back into the car and drove south, taking a quick look at an empty De Lautour's pool as I crossed the Waitahanui.

On the way south, I thought of Greg Kelly, angler, hunter, arms and ballistics expert, writer and bibliophile. I thought of his three major books, *The Gun in the Case, The Flies in My Hat* and *Gun in the Hills*; but because I am a fisherman I thought principally of the middle one and the author's special delight in Kakahi.

Greg moved from Taumarunui to his Shangri-la, Kakahi, in 1955 at age 67, with his second wife, Truda, after 20 years in the sports goods business followed by a further 20 at New Zealand Police Headquarters in Wellington as the country's ballistics expert.

If the ship taking him in 1905 at age 18 to the United States from a desperately unhappy childhood (he was orphaned at seven) in Victoria, Australia, had not put in, en route, to Milford Sound, New Zealand might never have known Greg Kelly.

That visit to Milford, giving the *Maheno's* passengers the opportunity to see soaring peaks, thick green bush and a fine waterfall, greatly impressed a young man jaded by the three-year drought he had just left in Victoria. Should he forget the United States and the job he hoped to get there with an arms company? A few days later, with the ship berthed at Lyttleton, he walked into the Cashmere Hills and liked what he saw there too. He decided he would stay in New Zealand.

He chose to begin his new life in Wellington, where he wasn't long in joining the Royal New Zealand Artillery — and apparently wasn't long in leaving it, either, for in 1907 he went north from Wellington to a job in the King Country.

Perfect days are hard to come by. This one, mantling Greg Kelly country, fulfilled every expectation. It began full of sunshine and blue sky, with a kind of light-hearted lilt to it; and it continued that way all day, and I was suitably glad, and humble, and thankful for the wonders it revealed.

Ever since a November day in 1990, when Cliff had introduced me to something of Greg Kelly's and Peter McIntyre's Kakahi, I had squirrelled away evocative mental pictures of the village, the narrow bush-tramway cutting leading to the Whakapapa, the river itself, and then the track alongside the Whakapapa to its confluence with the Wanganui. A little-used track it was, through blackberry and honeysuckle and scrub, and tall summer grasses and foxgloves. Steers luxuriated in the lush paddocks, and shining cuckoos called. I fished a slim brown nymph here and there, and may have had an offer in one place, but I responded too late.

In the evening, Cliff and I sat by the river above the old tramway bridge supports waiting for an evening rise, but it never came, so we drove back to the motel and reminisced over a whisky or two before sitting down to an excellent meal at the adjoining restaurant.

Today, 15 months later, the pasture land and trees of the Kakahi countryside you look down on as the valley unfolds below you, on the road in from State Highway 4, seemed darker, the trees more sombrely clad, especially those on the high forested hillside sloping back from the invisible Wanganui River below them.

But I have come too far too soon, too anxious to look again on the Kakahi that Greg Kelly and Peter McIntyre loved so well in the not-so-long-ago.

Let me begin just a little way upriver first, at Owhango, where a riverside reserve and walking tracks cater to picnickers and trampers. An old wooden bridge for the loggers of yesteryear spans the Whakapapa there, standing so much higher now above the water than it did before the power planners thrust the Tongariro Power Scheme upon us all.

I had come more or less on the spur of the moment from Taupo. I knew that I wanted to start picking up old threads which might lead me back to the reality of the fishing of days gone by. I would have to talk to one or two people at length, but that would have to be in the future, because there had been no time to make arrangements for today.

One thing I would do today was to fish a dry fly on Whakapapa waters in memory of Greg. Truda had likened the aloof cluster of dry flies on her husband's fishing hat to a collection of little snobs, and in deference to that description Greg had indeed written of them as little snobs in that happy fishing book of his.

He probably would not have known the dry fly I used that day, one of the Royal Wulffs I had bought at George Gatchell's. I wanted to trip it down fastish Whakapapa waters and bring trout up to it — if indeed trout were there to bring up.

The first pool above the old wooden bridge at Owhango is more of a run than a pool, but it curls and eddies, and today the clear water tumbled joyfully through it. The two Department of Conservation men I had talked with over lunch in the reserve had affirmed the presence of trout in the river. Later, the Kakahi storekeeper, Manu Lala, himself a trout-fisher, was to say the same, adding, though, that the fish were rather small. "To think we once used to put three-pounders back!" he lamented.

I expected the river to be colder than it was, so wet wading became pleasantly bearable. It must have been an intimidating river in days gone by if old water levels etched into high banks here and there are any indication.

First cast — first cast! — a fish came up for the little Royal Wulff. In 20 minutes four fish wanted it, but I only landed one, a small rainbow of no more than 250g. All came fast and furious to the fly, even the two that snatched at it in the slow edge of the lower eddy. I felt I should fish right up to the head of the pool, but for some reason the floating line kept on sucking under. I almost decided to try a weighted nymph thrown to land 2–3 metres beyond the start of the white water, but I persevered with the dry fly.

In 1959, someone wrote in the visitors' book at the Wilsons' Kakahi cottage, Te Whare Ra — the first fishing cottage built at Kakahi — that 30 years previously they had enjoyed "the best trout-fishing in the world" there. Greg, quoting this remark in a piece he wrote under the pseudonym Tangataroa for the Kakahi School Jubilee booklet, published that same year of 1959, said that it was probably an overstatement born of a nostalgic memory. All the same, he said the eruption of Mt Ruapehu in the mid-1940s was the cause of much of the current problem. It had dumped thousands of tonnes of ash on the Whakapapa glacier, and ever since, the ash had been washing into the stream, smothering fly-life. However, Greg went on to say, the standard of the fishing was still good: a weekend visitor to the Te Whare Ra cottage had taken four very good trout just below the junction of the Whakapapa and the Wanganui.

The following year, 1960, a publication marking Taumarunui's Jubilee, *Taumarunui Looks Forward*, printed an article by A.J. Ross also lauding the Whakapapa fishing above Kakahi. Compared with the Wanganui, the Whakapapa there was a fast, tough, roistering roughneck. Ways down to the river were few, but the angler still stood the chance of catching rainbows of 10lbs (4.5kg) or more; and if he were so blessed, he would have more than earned his fish. Said Mr Ross: "The Whakapapa is not for girls or the over-fifties . . ."

Well, here was a well-over-sixty fishing the Whakapapa today. Maybe it was just as well for him that the river was only a shadow, meanwhile, of its former self.

Two more Whakapapa fish that day came up swiftly to the Royal Wulff at Kakahi itself. I missed both of them. They lay in that attractive rippling run of water (100 metres or so upstream of the old concrete bridge supports) on which Cliff and I had willed an evening rise two years before, without result.

No doubt, in honour of another man of Kakahi, I ought to have fished a Kakahi Queen, but some doubt does remain about the identity of the originator of the pattern. We would all like to think, I'm sure, that Mr Basil Humphrey, the Kakahi postmaster from June 1916 to July 1924, developed the pattern. One authority attributes it to him unreservedly, but Greg Kelly is more cautious. True, in a piece he wrote in 1959, he did give the postmaster credit for the design, but in his book *The Flies in My Hat*, published in 1967, he attributes only the Twilight Beauty and the Jessie to Humphrey and Humphrey's small band of enthusiastic helpers.

Mrs Jessie Mont-Brown, for whom, as a 10-year-old, the Jessie was named, wrote to Greg some 50 years after the Twilight Beauty and Jessie had been designed. She vividly recalled the activities and history of the little group of enthusiasts, but on the matter of the Kakahi Queen she must have disappointed Greg. He wrote: "My correspondent adds that the Kakahi Queen was a very popular pattern in that district for many years, but does not claim that it was the work of the Humphrey coterie."

I believe Basil Humphrey probably enjoyed those eight years as postmaster at Kakahi a lot more than he enjoyed spells of duty elsewhere. True, he might have looked with the greatest pleasure on a subsequent transfer to an equally rewarding fishery, the brown trout fishery surrounding Gore; but Fate, or perhaps a non-fishing and sardonic head-office wallah, played him a cruel trick. His appointment to Gore in 1947 lasted only six months, and only the first month of the six was open for trout-fishing. Maybe he made up for lost time, though, by remaining in Gore once his job there finished; his next Post Office job did not take effect until the first of April the following year. Did he take long-service leave? And if he did, did he take some or all of it in Gore's brown trout country?

Someone may yet discover more about the trout-fishing postmaster who Greg Kelly first introduced to the angling public in 1967. No doubt Basil Humphrey fished Kakahi Queens, Twilight Beauties and Jessies for years once his little group of enthusiasts had brought him the natural flies from which the artificials were then designed. Undoubtedly, too, because so many pools and runs and unexpected little waterways crossed and surrounded it, making it a wonderfully exciting place — and it being so close to the village too — the Kakahi postmaster would have loved The Island.

The Island! Thirty years after Basil Humphrey, when the river still ran magnificently from the mountains, and the old bush tramway bridge to

The Island still carried trucks hauling logs from the bush, the Kellys and the McIntyres and the Haggitts joyously fished and picnicked all around. The Island, with its familiar tracks and intricate waterways, and the countryside about it, yielded all manner of delights for people who couldn't abide the confines and pretences and turmoil of city life. What times they had in those truly good old days of Kakahi!

Nowadays, if you haven't a horse, you have to wade across to The Island. I took the rod with me, and stuffed binoculars and camera and two camera lenses into the pack. Only when I found myself waist deep in fastish water flowing over biggish boulders did I begin to regret taking vulnerable precious things with me. One of these days I shall start a river crossing quite dry and finish it quite wet. Luckily, today wasn't to be that day. I really must buy some lightweight plastic containers with waterproof closures, and carry binoculars, camera gear and other water-sensitive items in those rather than continue to put my trust, pathetically, in an it-can't-happen-to-me attitude.

If you know Greg Kelly's *The Flies in My Hat* and Peter McIntyre's *Kakahi*, you will want to explore The Island. It lies directly across from the track which deposits you where The Cutting peters out not far from the river. Behind you, on a fine, dry day, such as that with which I had been blessed, the straight road into The Cutting will only just be recovering from the car's passage. Fine yellow dust all along the way billows up in choking clouds. The dust cloud caught me up and gently settled on the car as I stopped briefly to contemplate a call at the Kelly's old home, Mar Lodge. But I went on my way. Another day would come.

Then I was into The Cutting, shut in by walls reaching high above, and trees at the top touching hands across the divide. Were there glow-worms still to be seen there? Greg and daughter Cassie, going home in the dark from fishing the evening rise, would stop in wonder at the little groups of lights along The Cutting. But Truda, Cassie's stepmother, would already be worrying about them, so they could not linger long. Greg once fell and broke his glasses. That had been a bad moment for Truda. She didn't like him going duck-shooting, either; she was afraid he would die in his mai mai. In the end, her nervousness at night in that little cottage of theirs high above the river, on the site Cassie herself had chosen for it, forced a move to surroundings less fearful for Truda in 1963. It nearly broke Greg's heart. The day they left Mar Lodge, Truda cried and cried, knowing how he felt.

Cassie says Greg named the cottage after a famous Scottish hunting

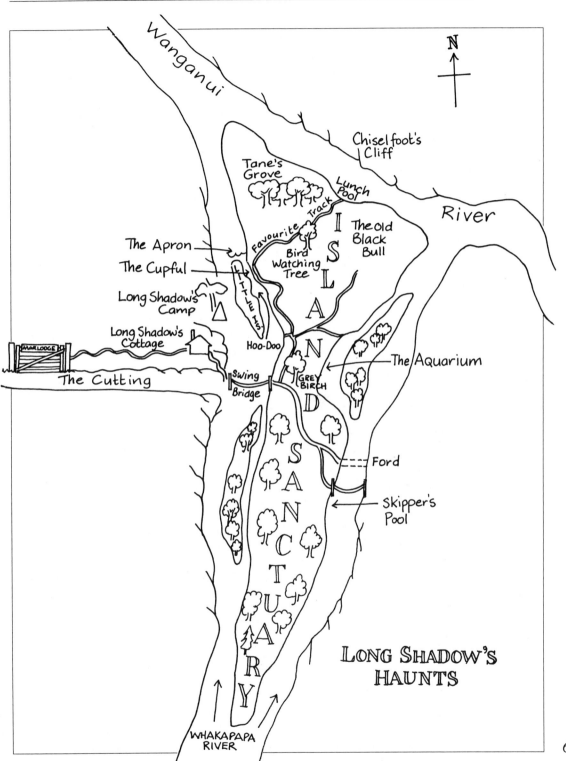

Wanganui

River

N

Chisel foot's
Cliff

Tane's
Grove

Lunch
Pool

The Apron

Favourite Track

The Cupful

Bird
Watching
Tree

The Old
Black
Bull

I
S
L
A
N
D

Long Shadow's
Camp

LITTLE IS.

Long Shadow's
Cottage

Hoo-Doo

MAR LODGE

Swing
Bridge

GREY
BIRCH

The Aquarium

The Cutting

S
A
N
C
T
U
A
R
Y

Ford

Skipper's
Pool

Long Shadow's
Haunts

WHAKAPAPA
RIVER

lodge. There is a Scottish salmon fly of the same name, of course, named for that same lodge.

I thought the presence of the Department of Conservation sign on The Island quite strange. It faces the "mainland" across the river and tells you that you are looking at the Kakahi Island Scenic Reserve. Perhaps the law demands that land gazetted public reserve shall be signposted accordingly, irrespective of whether or not the public can take advantage of it. In this case, the only way to get to The Island dryshod is by horse or boat. So what is the attraction of The Island now? Why do some of the locals indeed cross to and from it on horseback? Why were two farm trikes puttering about near the DoC sign? Where was the cheerful Maori on horseback headed who passed me on the island track leading upriver? I walked some distance after him, but could not follow further because time was running out for me that day.

Perhaps it was no longer an island? Perhaps the shrunken Whakapapa, victim of the Tongariro Power Scheme, had forsaken the shallower waterways on the far side?

The map Truda drew of that wonderful island sanctuary, and the stories she used to weave for Cassie Blair's small son, tell of a time when the Kelly family enjoyed idyllic summer holidays there. She titled the map Long Shadow's Haunts. Long Shadow was the English translation of the Maori name Tangataroa, under which Greg wrote for the old *New Zealand Fishing and Shooting Gazette* and occasionally for other publications.

And the names on the map! They conjure up the simple joys of long ago. Chiselfoot's Cliff lies across the Wanganui opposite the Lunch Pool, which is reached by the Favourite Track. There's the Cupful Pool, The Aquarium, Skipper's Pool (was this one named for Frank Yerex?), Long Shadow's Camp, the Bird-Watching Tree, the Hoodoo Pool, and Greg's much-loved Apron Pool.

What joyful days they had, at Kakahi, in the wonderful world of long ago.

Happy in my eccentricity

This evening at home I read an article by a man who thinks I need certifying. He did not actually say, "John Parsons needs certifying because if he goes fishing he doesn't mind if he doesn't catch a fish," but he lumped all of us together whose vision of fishing gets clouded at times by things other than fish. If we admit to enjoying all the sights and sounds of a day by the water and honestly don't mind if we fail to catch a fish, we need certifying as insane.

We can't really call ourselves fishermen until we have deliberately read all we can about fishing, hired all the videos we can about fishing, and put into practice as often as possible all we have learnt. So says the enthusiast.

That way (provided we catch fish, of course) we shall avoid the penalties of failure. The ignominy of defeat, the ridicule the family heaps upon us, the shame of being beaten by mere fish, the inferiority complex that so constricts our maturity, no longer shall be ours.

One day, when that young man's wife and family and friends finally lose interest in what he catches, and, hopefully, he learns that fishing is not a game of rugby, to be won at all costs, but a recreation to be enjoyed, we shall welcome his release into the kindlier world he has denied himself for so long.

Just now it sounds as though he performs a haka before he marches grimly to each confrontation with the enemy. Is he perhaps a fishing guide? That would explain a lot. Fishing guides desperately need fish. After all, if anyone must catch fish, a client must. At the end of a day without fish, a client won't want a guide the next day who speaks chiefly of the beauty of Nature. Guiding is a business, and a business in which fishing pleasure for the guide should play a minor role.

If he is a guide, our writer no doubt believes, with most of his fellow guides, that only catching fish really matters. Everything else is for the birds. He will admit, though, if he is honest, to a necessity for clients to take their fish from clean waters in an unspoilt natural environment. If so, that speaks well for the guiding fraternity, which surely knows the importance, especially for anglers from overseas, of the attainable beautiful, clean green, New Zealand trout-fishing experience.

So many anglers too, who espouse the strictly literal message of going fishing, also say that nothing matters but the fish. If you go fishing, they say, you're not much of an angler if you fail to come home with fish. Forget about the birds and the buttercups. Concentrate on fish. Get your priorities right.

I get the worrying impression that they couldn't care less about the settings of their fishing. They would be equally happy, it seems, hooking fish in waters confined within hectares of sterile green concrete, as in hooking them in settings shaped by the passage of time and the changing face and moods of Nature.

I feel especially sad tonight about the plight of the young man who wrote the article because today, of all days, I qualified even more comprehensively for certification as insane, and I'm not in the least repentant.

Out there, fishing, I told myself firmly now and again that I had not come to steep myself in nostalgia. After all, I do hope to fish the river for a good many years to come. But I had not explored so far upstream for three years, and, as I went through the familiar places, I remembered fish in this pool and that, and Bryn's beaming face here and there, and Bill being bested by a fish that went the wrong way round an island, and Brian settling down in the warm grass with his hat over his eyes for an after-lunch siesta while the rest of us wandered off upstream.

Those wonderful days are past. But today was just as wonderful; and I mean, full of wonder: the wonder of a hot summer's day tempered by a small breeze; the buttercups rubbing shoulders with seeding thistles as though spring had jumped straight into autumn; toetoe plumes along the stream, dipping and fanning in the breeze like flags along the street when the Queen goes by. The wonder of yellow vetch and golden ragwort among tall seeding summer grasses; the swift dry rustle of wings as a big dragon-fly settled on my hat; the fernbirds that haunted me throughout the day, calling and tick-ticking their displeasure at my intrusion; the two white geese on an island; the sudden flurry of swallows crisscrossing the sky just above my head; and then the wonder of a lazily feeding brown trout patrolling the smooth tail of the next pool.

Such wonders, on a day bright with sunshine and blue and white skies, wonders capped by a 1.5kg brown trout which I saw I could put a fly to without trouble, fill my whole being with gratitude for the natural world around. I could no more ignore the settings of my fishing than cast a fly to the moon.

Watching that brown trout moving steadily here and there, deftly fielding the insects being bowled at him, I knew my day would be the richer for his undoing, but I also knew that if I hooked and lost him, or sent him off in a fright, the smooth skin of my day's enjoyment would suffer only the mildest of scratches. If I hooked him and managed to land him, I would release him anyway.

I wonder what the young writer would have done about that fish. On the one hand, wouldn't he have needed the corpse of the fish to prove himself once again to wife and children? On the other hand, if he were a guide, would he not be dedicated to the philosophy (and the self-protective practice) of catch and release? What if, though, as a guide, he practised catch and release, but his children were too young to accept the philosophy?

The fish wouldn't look at the chubby, nondescript nymph I threw up to him from my position precariously perched halfway down a high bank, some feet above the river. What about a Keith Simpson Dark Whisker dry fly? I had watched the trout twice come to the surface and once take something from it. But no, he did not want a Dark Whisker. Sorry, Keith.

I tied on a small Coch y Bonddu of my own tying, and sent it up to him. The trouble was, I couldn't see it on the water. When the fish turned round and took something off the surface roughly where I thought my fly might be, I waited a couple of seconds and speculatively lifted the point of the rod.

Indeed, he had taken the Coch y Bonddu, and he rushed for shelter.

Shelter on this river is the undercut bank, and undercut banks are legion. He found three in 30 seconds. The third was home, I fancy, a deep hole under the trailing leaves of a considerable toetoe bush. I left him there while I lowered myself into the river and crossed over, then I pulled him downstream, and he came round in front of me, turning upstream. The landing net already lay in the water, but oddly enough the fish appeared not to notice it, not even when I pushed it in after him as he went under the bank alongside me. I pushed the net further in, telling myself I was an idiot if I thought I could catch him like that. But, lo and behold, he was in the net when I withdrew it, a beautiful, thickly spotted brown trout.

The fly conveniently came away while he threshed around, so I did not have to handle him at all, but emptied him gently back into the river.

Then it was lunchtime, and suddenly I spotted another trout. I would watch him while I ate lunch on the bank some metres downstream, but first I would have to clear a few thistles out of the way.

They came up easily. It was like pulling up tomato stakes. I guess they surrendered so meekly because the valley has been so long without rain. It is a pity about the presence of thistles. I am quite sure they have only recently become established. Luckily, no blackberry has yet appeared.

Lunch over, I flipped a Pheasant Tail nymph to the trout, and at that very moment a breeze blew the line aside, over the fish, and it went from that place like greased lightning. Sanctuary, again, turned out to be an undercut bank below a spread of toetoe.

Further up, having given the two white geese a wide berth in case they blundered off upstream ahead of me (what on earth were they doing there anyway, so far from habitation?), I spotted a fish feeding in a quick, rippling run of water colourful with brown and grey-green stones. The trout glimmered greenly here and there, turned on his side once to take something from a stone (not my small caddis imitation), and suddenly was there no longer.

Maybe I ought to have climbed out of the river and up the high bank at the next pool, to try and spot a trout. But I don't think the exercise would have greatly influenced the result. It's a pool with a dogleg bend, deepening quickly, burrowing under overhanging flax and toetoe to round a corner and then slow down along a sheer high bank. From the track high above you can usually watch a trout feeding, sometimes two.

A deep expanse of soft pumice sand fills the inside angle of the dogleg, and it was across this expanse that I began casting a Hare and Copper nymph into the fast water at the head of the pool. Third time down the line-end stopped, and a trout was on, and then off, as quickly as that. Pity. But that loss couldn't sour my day, couldn't drive me into despair, couldn't make me wonder how on earth I would break it to the children . . .

You will never know all there is to know about catching trout, but by all means learn as much as you can; after all, you go fishing to catch fish, sure you do, but if you don't catch fish — and even the most expert don't always — give thanks for the wonderful world around you, and enjoy every moment, every sight and sound of it, while you can — and while it lasts.

As Eric Taverner once observed: "Any man who goes to the river, takes what he can catch, and cares naught for 'countrey contentments', as Gervase Markham described them more than three centuries ago, is a pot-fisher and unworthy of the name of angler."

Wild trout in natural surroundings gleam like gems in precious settings. For me it's the settings just as much as the trout that invest the hours spent fishing with countless satisfactions.

Jack's Rotongaio

Jack is an exceptionally talented fly-fisher. He takes his fishing very seriously indeed, and he also loves the settings into which it takes him. Because of health reasons in the mid-1980s, he concentrated on the smaller lakes of the region. He had to put behind him his once long and strenuous days on Tongariro with the upstream nymph.

For some time, Lake Otamangakau became almost an obsession; and then he found Rotongaio, the shallow, spring-fed lagoon just south of Waitahanui.

With characteristic thoroughness, Jack first explored the lagoon with boat and plumb line. He charted all his soundings. He found holes up to 20 metres deep. So much of the shoreline dropped so steeply into 3 metres of water that, although a few places could be fished wading, he knew that a boat would be the only way to fish the lagoon successfully.

This conclusion suited Jack very well until the day he tipped out. He managed to clamber back in, and spent the next two hours slowly and carefully bailing out with an empty beer can until he could reach gingerly forward and pull up the anchor. He continued to boat-fish the lagoon regularly once he had designed and fitted a flotation tube, full of polystyrene beads, to encircle the boat just below the gunwhale. The boat was now unsinkable. Furthermore, it could not be tipped over.

Jack became a Rotongaio enthusiast, happy to pay the couple of dollars or so each time he wanted to take car and boat onto the property and fish

69

the lagoon.

The old man seemingly in charge of the place didn't want outboards on boats and didn't allow trolling. That suited Jack fine. He would row quietly to his fishing and enjoy a lake free from the sounds and smells of boat engines.

Not surprisingly, because he is such a fine angler, Jack's fishing at Rotongaio was well rewarded. Using small nymphs, as he had done at Lake Otamangakau, he commonly hooked at least five fish on every visit, sometimes many more. Several fish have broken him. Oddly, he could catch only rainbows there, but when he told a friend about the place the man went there and caught a 3.5kg brown.

Obviously, Jack treasures his Rotongaio memories — of days disturbed only by the plunge of big fish into the raupo, the calling of bellbirds, the adventuring ducklings around the boat, the slow gait of pukekos, the flight of bitterns.

Then came the talk of a big international hotel on Rotongaio's shores and, worse still, a marina. Hell, said Jack, if they put a marina in they'll have to dredge the outlet into Lake Taupo. And you know what that would mean to the fishery? Finish!

Jack asked me what I thought. Should he keep the place to himself for as long as he could? Or should he tell the world all about that wonderful fishery just 15 minutes away from Taupo, where big fish were always present, and where a man could find a sheltered anchorage in any weather and still fish in comfort?

If he told the world about all the good things at Rotongaio, anglers would surely flock to the place, and wouldn't they then get behind a campaign to oppose the development?

I told Jack to keep the place to himself, to enjoy it while he could. A few other trout-fishers also frequented the lake. Whether they felt the same as he did, or were not greatly concerned about the development, seemed to me of no consequence. The land was Maori land. It looked as though the years of paid holiday-making in tents and caravans on the property, as well as all the years of paid fishing of the lagoon, were almost at an end. It was sad, as all similar so-called progress is sad.

That was eight years ago. Nothing has changed, except that the place is closed to the public. No hotel was built and no marina constructed. If you try to make a sentimental journey into the property briefly to relive cherished camping or fishing memories, you are likely to be confronted and bundled out by young men with guns.

A *ranger's lot . . .*

Jerry Potts was always busy. You would be busy, too, if you were harbour master, traffic inspector, a member of the local Airport Committee, forestry ranger, supervisor of a historic cemetery, and host to all the VIPs Head Office sent up to you from Wellington to take out hunting or fishing. And all that without doing your real job, which was to be a no-nonsense, full-time field officer for the Department of Internal Affairs in Taupo.

If you were lucky, you might find time occasionally, but only occasionally, to hunt and fish yourself.

Jerry Potts was lucky. He did indeed find time, especially in the early days of his incumbency. His parish extended all the way from Taupo to Tokaanu, and in the beginning years from 1927 — before the department, no doubt grudgingly, supplied a car — he would travel on horseback between the two outposts of his domain. Quail were everywhere, sometimes in coveys of up to 400 birds. It would be a poor day that saw him come home without at least a score of quail for the pot.

Sometimes he would shoot with three friends at the Motuoapa Swamp. Judge Osler, Tom and Archie Banks (the brothers in charge of the prison farms close to Turangi) and he would have great sport there.

The journeying to and from Tokaanu on horseback, and the duties he had to perform between the two settlements, would often take longer than Jerry Potts expected, and he was always glad on those occasions of the department's cottage at Jellicoe Point, his halfway house for many a night.

When Jerry went to Taupo in 1927, he reckoned there were only 92 pakehas living there. Was that the year when, he said, the whole place could have been bought for £2,000 ($4,000), and lakefront sections sold for 7 shillings and sixpence (75c) an acre?

He and his wife Queenie bought themselves an acre where Tui Oaks Motel now stands, on the corner of Lake Terrace and Tui Street, and they built a home there with a large plate-glass picture window from which the magnificence of the lake and the mountains was seen to pleasing effect.

A macrocarpa hedge with an archway cut into it over the gate lay between the house and the road. Perhaps that view through the archway and over the open gate was the one the English artist Lamorna Birch chose to paint of the prospect from the Potts' home, on his visit to Taupo in 1937.

71

I often wonder where that painting is today. Jerry Potts' daughter-in-law Margaret doesn't know. She feels that perhaps her late husband, Ian, passed it on, with other things from the house, to members of Jerry's family when the old man died in 1970 and the house was demolished or moved elsewhere.

That painting is one of three I know Lamorna Birch painted at Taupo during the artist's visit. Did he paint more? He must have come to Taupo to fish, for he was a very keen and very good fly-fisher. Unquestionably, because of the two pictures he completed at Huka Lodge — and possibly two signs there, each featuring a trout — he spent some time there with the owners, Alan and Leila Pye. His painting of the Potts' view over the lake to the mountains may well have been an expression of thanks for being looked after by the ranger and his wife. Were his paintings around Huka Lodge — one of the lodge from over the river, and one of a Waikato River pool close by — commissioned by Alan Pye? Or were they payment for his stay at the lodge? The two paintings were in the possession of Leila Pye when she died. She left one of them to her nephew and one to her doctor.

Those years of the 1930s were as pleasurable as they were busy for Jerry Potts. Both Queenie and he came to love the lake and the landscape at Taupo. Queenie liked her trout-fishing as much as Jerry liked his. He may have shied away from having his photograph taken on fishing excursions with his VIPs, for I have yet to find a picture of him, but Queenie was more forthcoming. At least she appeared in several of the early Taupo trout-fishing photographs, often in a big hat, and often holding up a large rainbow trout, but of course she might have been as reluctant to face a camera as Jerry, and only fell victim to the photographer because lady anglers were not all that common in those days, particularly lady anglers who looked so charming and yet so clearly knew all about catching trout.

Like many other trout-fishers in the neighbourhood, Queenie would have tried to make an end of Hughie, the big brown trout that at one time used to feed in the shallows along the edge of the lake off Tui Street. But no-one could catch him.

"One day," said Jerry, "a bit of a boy went down and started to fish. He threw his line in and it fell in a tangled heap.

"Hughie came along and grabbed the fly. There he was, hooked at last, and the boy managed to drag him in. He was a nice 12-pounder — caught, in the end, more or less by accident."

The largest fish Jerry ever saw was an 8.2kg fish taken in the Waitahanui

rip by old Awhi Northcroft. That would have fallen for a wet fly, or lure, the usual kind of fly for the rip; but only a short way away, on the Waikato River, Jerry for two years delighted in fishing the dry fly at dusk for the free-rising rainbows of the Huka Pool, above Huka Falls.

Captain Arthur Richardson discovered the dusk rise of the big rainbows there in 1928, and quickly invited Jerry to go along with him one night to see for himself. The wildlife ranger at once became an enthusiast. The Captain and he had two years of extraordinary fishing there before the Pyes established the Huka Fishing Lodge on the property.

The dusk fishers found that the English dry fly was not big enough to hold a fish when it went across the river. The current bellied the line and the hook pulled out, so they tied their own flies on larger hooks.

"One night," said Jerry, "I watched Captain Richardson cast three times. The first cast he hooked a six-pounder. He changed his fly, cast again, and landed an eight-pounder. He changed his fly once more and got a 12-pounder.

"All that on a dry fly in three casts in the Huka Pool!"

Much of my information about Jerry Potts comes from his daughter-in-law, and much from an unsigned article about him printed in the Taupo Centenary edition of the *Taupo Times* in 1969. Jerry died in 1970, two years before I went to live in Taupo, and years later he had become just another distant, legendary, almost fairy-tale character. Then I happened to mention him to a longtime resident of Taupo, Dr Bill Drake, and Jerry Potts suddenly became a real person. The doctor, as a small boy in 1934 or 1935, recalled being by the slipway in the harbour one day and seeing the ranger upending a milk churn into the shallow water there. Jerry would have been wearing the green porkpie hat with which Bill Drake always associates him, and smoking the inevitable cigarette.

The boy could see little fish pouring out of the milk churn and swimming around.

"What are those, Mr Potts?"

"They're smelt, lad. To feed the trout."

Bill Drake didn't know it at the time, but he saw one of the first — perhaps the very first — consignments of smelt from Rotorua being turned into Lake Taupo in an attempt to establish a much-needed new food for the trout.

The experiment succeeded. The introduced forage fish *Retropinna retropinna* has been the salvation of the Taupo fishery. How appropriate that Jerry Potts, wildlife ranger and self-styled official jack of all trades at

Taupo, should have played his part in establishing the little fish that, 60 years later, continues to preserve the fame of Taupo trout.

Skues would have been disgusted

Have you ever caught a trout with a tangled ball of roots in its stomach? I have, twice. But it wasn't a tangled ball of roots at all.

Harry and Judy had picked almost 3kg of luscious late-autumn blackberries somewhere between the Rat Country and Bishop's that day. I'm not sure that Harry had fished at all but, all accoutred in fishing vest, he was driving the car that stopped alongside me as I trudged down the road towards Bishop's. No, he had no fish to show, but they had picked a whole lot of blackberries, Judy said 6lb, and they were on their way home.

I recalled picking a whole lot myself, within a stone's throw of where we chatted, one March day a couple of years before, on an occasion of no fish. Perhaps I might be forced to do the same again today? The afternoon was already far advanced, and I hadn't even begun to fish. In the old days, and in the eyes of members of the family not wholly sympathetic to hours of misspent time, bringing something home from a fishing trip went a little way towards begrudging acceptance of one's idiocy. I once went home with a cabbage.

Would it be blackberries again today? Margaret and Michael love blackberry and apple pie.

I went down the long, steep bank with the grey shingle slipping and rattling like scree under my jungle boots. On the way, I decided never to leave it so late in the day again to go fishing, unless I wanted to try and prove something about an evening rise. First day of New Zealand standard time it was, and already the prospect of a short twilight was knocking at the door of the afternoon. I love to start in the mornings; not too early, mind, because the steep sides of the winding valley keep a lot of the river in shadow for some hours. If you start reasonably early, though, you enjoy the day more, knowing there are hours and hours of bliss ahead.

What was left of today hindered rather than helped. I felt I ought to hurry. And then I thought, "Why hurry? You can always get out of the river past the third bend instead of plunging on to Winstone's. Yes?"

I might be forced to get out of the water early anyway. This was hill country, hinting suddenly and decidedly at early winter after Taupo's warmer temperature. When I'd got out of the car I'd had to reach quickly for a jersey. Nevertheless, I had decided to wade wet. The river appeared lowish, and clear, and I trusted it not to be too cold. And it wasn't.

The new pool below Bishop's brought a trout to the Hare and Copper nymph straightaway. The fish flashed a silver side at me as it spat the fly out. Ten, maybe 15, casts later, a strong and energetic fish took hold. I stopped it short of the log under which it plainly intended to burrow, so it about-turned and rushed past me downstream and out of the pool, tearing line off the reel. I coaxed it from behind a rock in a fast run, and drew it into the shallows.

That fish would be living today if it had not taken the nymph right down, a circumstance which in my experience is extremely rare. I killed it. Later, at home, I found only a skerrick or two of food in its stomach. I did not count as food the loose mass of rootlets I also found there. It was like a couple of metres of tangled, hollow, two-tone brown monofilament. I broke one or two pieces off. They stretched some way before breaking. What sort of rootlets were they?

The fish in the deep tail of the corner pool, under the rock face, had the laugh on me. I knew very well that if there were one there, my first cast would be my last chance of deceiving it. I also knew just where the take would come, if it came at all. I knew too, after making the cast, that I ought to have been retrieving line faster than I was.

Lightning-fast the take came, pulling the line-end upstream. Nothing was there when my reflexes responded.

Ominously, nothing intercepted the nymph in the two small pools above the corner pool. The tricky crossing directly upstream of the corner pool — tricky even in the low-water conditions of that day — brought quite enough heart into mouth without the added trauma of a seeming absence of fish in two places which have practically never failed me in the past.

Late-afternoon light silvered the current rippling down towards me, and because of the perceptible imminence of dusk, I left the river. It was already dim inside the green caverns between the old pongas and young bush and occasional beeches. This was the way Bryn and I had gone from the river back to the car one happy Boxing Day, along the faint old track high over the water.

Next day, Don Forsyth and Clive Howard-Williams of the DSIR in Taupo peered at the 12cm sections of thin brown rootlets I took into the laboratory. They pronounced them animal, not vegetable. The tangle of strands turned out to be a collection of hairworms, sometimes called Gordian worms; not nematodes (the parasitic worms which you sometimes find encysted on the stomach walls of trout), but nematomorphs, which are parasitic also, but not on trout.

Although not uncommon, little appears to be known about nematomorphs. Professor B.J. Marples, in his book *An Introduction to Freshwater Life in New Zealand*, offers what to this layman is rather contradictory information about hairworms. On the one hand he speaks of nematomorphs as being found freely in the water, and says they lay large numbers of eggs which apparently encyst themselves on vegetation "and when eaten by some insect . . . bore their way from the gut into the body". On the other hand, he says that the usual host is a grasshopper. The worm grows into a fully-formed creature in the body of the grasshopper, forces its way out, and takes up life in the water. The mind boggles.

Anyway, it is nice to know that the fit, pink, sturdy 1.2kg rainbow that had succumbed to my Hare and Copper had not acted as host to a parasitic worm. It had merely found the sluggish bundle of hairworms and gobbled them up.

I wish I had not broken bits off the tangle, but had unravelled the bundle and counted the constituent worms. If there is a next time for me, I shall know better. I shall also know — and you ought to know too — that the Auckland Museum and the Dominion Museum are likely to be most grateful for specimens of nematomorphs, whether you find them skulking in a backwater, swimming about in trout, or hopping around in amphibious grasshoppers.

Strangely, on the very next occasion I fished in the vicinity of Bishop's, I caught another rainbow with a stomach full of hairworms. I had never, over a period of 40 years of fly-fishing for trout, taken a fish with nematomorphs inside it, before the one I caught in March. And here was a second.

This one came from Bishop's. It was the second fish I landed from the pool. The first was around half a kilo in weight. The second was twice as big, and I kept it to replace the deep-frozen trout we had recently given away.

I had gone fishing at 3 o'clock — again, far too late in the day, really — but the weather was hot and clammy, and I suddenly yearned for an hour or two of wet wading in a small stream. Besides, I wanted to try Juriaan's Goldhead flies, which had arrived in a letter of his from Holland only a few days before.

From Acacia Bay, the sky towards Hawke's Bay was filled with misty

77

cloud. The hills were indistinct under the heat haze. As I drove east, the patch of sky to which I was heading seemed to grow more and more ominously grey. It's very often the case that the weather in Taupo differs considerably from the weather not too far away to the east. It rather looked as though I might be in for a drenching. The still and sultry afternoon had almost the feel of an imminent thunderstorm about it.

The weighty Goldhead with the ginger body fastened to three objects in the first five minutes: my right ear, the landing net hanging down my back, and then, temporarily, a trout about twice as long as my middle finger. That was the extent of my fishing in the pool below Bishop's. Juriaan's Goldheads are not unmanageably heavy, but almost so on the 5-weight line I prefer to use on small rivers.

I moved up to Bishop's, and in 10 minutes had hooked and landed two rainbows. Interestingly, although I used the Goldhead — a blackish-bodied version this time — as the heavy tail fly, and an indeterminate, small, grey wet fly 60cm above it on a dropper, both fish took the Goldhead.

The second had me in all kinds of bother. I tried to net it at the tail of

the pool, where the water gathers strength for its rush down to the next pool. It shot into the net most obligingly, but then it shot out again, before arrowing downstream between my legs. At first I didn't know what had happened. Where was the fish? I couldn't work out why the rod appeared to be on the point of breaking. The top joint was under water and bent in a semicircle pointing downstream. I reversed my grip on the rod, holding it halfway along, with the butt pointing away upstream. The current was too strong to risk stepping over the rod, so I guided the tip through my legs, then fed the whole jolly rod through, with the fish bucking and prancing around in the rapids behind me. What a performance! I expected the hook to tear out, or the tippet to give, at any moment; but I managed to steer the fish into slower water at the side of the river, and land it.

The steep bank dropping down to the river was thick with daisies. I have never seen such a multitude on the bank. As I went up it on the way back to the car, I looked down at the trout I carried, and was most interested to see a thick, brown length of live "monofilament" climbing out of its mouth. Another hairworm! Back at the car, I pulled the thing clear of the fish. It was only about 30cm long.

A whole lot more awaited me when I cleaned the fish at home; but, as the other had been, this one too was a fit, pink-fleshed fish, and would no doubt taste as good. Strangely, the worms in the stomach made no movement when I took them out, washed them and poked them into a clear-plastic film canister, and yet the first one had been definitely alive when I pulled it out of the trout's mouth before driving back to Taupo.

The obvious explanation for the nematomorphs' presence around Bishop's is that the river and its banks and insect hosts upstream of the pool must suit the lifestyle of this odd, supposedly rare, parasitic worm — a worm which, but for hungry trout, might otherwise think it had found nirvana there.

Mindful of the DSIR's earlier suggestion that if ever I "caught" more hairworms the Auckland or Dominion Museum could well be interested in receiving them, I took them into the Taupo laboratory of the department's Division of Marine and Freshwater Research. There they would be properly preserved and labelled for whatever future might be in store for them.

Autumn

Enigmatic Otamangakau

Lake Otamangakau keeps itself mostly to itself, or so I find. Like a poker machine, and poker-faced with it, it swallows small fortunes of angling time. Whole days can go by utterly unrewarded except for the worried duets of paradise ducks, the changing faces of the mountains across the way, and the quartering flight of hunting harrier hawks.

Quite suddenly, Otamangakau will pay out. The one-armed bandit relents. Often the win transcends your wildest dreams. The reel screams and a great trout leaps frantically from the waves 50 metres away and crashes back, and leaps again, and again. A 10-pounder, at least!

You hang on and pray. If you're wading, and if it's summer time, when weed growth is strong, you may lose the fish. People in boats and float-tubes lose fish too, even though they can usually pull up armfuls of weed in search of the particular thicket in which their fish has chosen to sulk.

Late summer finds the weed-beds wilting. Wading anglers' chances of landing fish rise and rise as the weeks wear on into autumn and the weed-beds fall and fall.

When I fished there late in March, though, *Elodea canadensis* seemed as vigorous as ever. The lake level had fallen, and in some places I could wade right into the edges of *Elodea* beds and watch the big pulmonate snails ponderously grazing the tall green spires. No-one noticing the size of those snails will wonder at the bulk of so many Lake Otamangakau fish, or fail to diagnose the gritty, grating kind of noise which comes from a massaged big-fish stomach.

In the light of this, should the angler offer only snail imitations? You might think that snails would be a logical choice, but those who catch fish at The Big O know that, unless it is midsummer and cicadas or damselfly nymphs feature largely on the menu, imitations of chironomid larvae and pupae account for the majority of rod-caught fish.

I cheated. Well, I abandoned thoughts of chironomids. This meant, however, that I handicapped myself rather than cheated, but if you could have fished with me throughout the two hours I stood in McGivern's Bay on the morning of the second day of a rare four-day fishing holiday, based in Turangi, you would have scoffed at any idea of handicapping. In those two hours I encountered four fish.

To those who are not Lake Otamangakau anglers, four fish in two hours may not be cause for celebration, or even mention, but to me, those four encounters came suspiciously — even indecently — quickly. After the fourth, I looked apprehensively around. The lake's warm response to my presence was completely out of character. Was it preparing me for a series of misfortunes? Would I end up up-ended in the shallows on the bay's treacherous mudstone shore? Perhaps I would break my precious carbon-fibre rod, tear a great hole in my chest waders, drop a box of flies into deep water?

None of these things happened. The lake affected total indifference. The flies alone had wrought that quartet of small miracles; the flies and the fortuitous presence — or, more likely, passage — of several fish. And the second fly I used was new at Otamangakau. I'll guarantee that it had never been seen there before, either by fish or man.

True, the first fish I encountered took a slim caddis imitation and spat it out before I could make lasting contact, but I'm not really counting that one. After that, nothing kept on happening for such a long time that I replaced the caddis with my one and only Hedgehogger.

In the beginning, some weeks before, there were two Hedgehoggers, a present from their inventor, Gil Brandeis, but a Waipunga rainbow stole the first one away. The second one deceived a second rainbow in the same Waipunga pool within five minutes of the first. I landed that fish, and so retained the fly.

Three McGivern's Bay fish fancied the Hedgehogger at its Lake Otamangakau debut, but only one wanted to keep it. And keep it she did, but just for the 10 minutes she leapt and thrashed and tussled before coming ashore and into the net. I believe she weighed somewhere around 4kg. In the net, which is a big one, she was very big, bigger than the 3.7kg rainbow I took out of Jaws' Bay some years ago, but smaller than the 4.5kg fish which now hangs on my workroom wall. The other two fish sampled the Hedgehogger briefly, and just weren't there when I went to drive the hook home.

Those four expressions of interest in two hours naturally persuaded me into spending more time at the Big O than I had intended over my four days' holiday. That change of mind was abetted by a conviction, probably quite unsound, that no worthwhile fish lay in the Tongariro where I wanted to fish it. One of those places rejoices in the name of Boulder Reach — well, in my Tongariro vocabulary it does — and I had fished Boulder Reach quite unsuccessfully during the afternoon of my arrival at Turangi.

Admittedly, my first upstream cast brought a quick response; so did the second and the third. Three fish in three casts, especially if they are the first casts you make on a fishing holiday, call almost for a champagne celebration, but all three, and subsequently two more Boulder Reach fish, were barely 15cm long. I slackened line, and they all came off, thanks to the accommodating nature of the doctored hook, a black size 10 Partridge, straight-eyed, long-shank sedge or caddis hook. I had tied five gold-ribbed *Aoteapsyche colonica* imitations on my Partridge hooks on the eve of my holiday. Three characteristics of the hook interested me. First the colour, black; second the straight eye, an eye neither turned up nor turned down; and thirdly an oh-so-neat barb (very close to the point of the hook itself), which broke off, leaving no trace whatsoever, under gentle pressure from a pair of pliers.

Perhaps if I had persevered, searching several deeper places with the caddis, I might have brought bigger fish to the hook, but having thoroughly combed the Cliff Pool deeps for half an hour without a touch, I made my way back to the Red Hut Bridge. That afternoon, not a soul disturbed my solitude. It was good to be there alone for a change. It wouldn't be very long before autumn rains and cooler weather sent fish upriver and anglers after them.

Just now, the Tongariro flowed moderately low and very clear to the lake. Only a couple of weeks or so ago it had roared furiously down, 3 metres above its normal level. At such times of raging flood, the dull roar of rolling boulders is unbelievably loud.

The banks of Boulder Reach had suffered. Here and there, slender manuka and kowhai lay half-collapsed down sections that had been undercut, inhibiting the upstream cast. Where I could, I took the leaning stems out with the little folding saw I carry. It's a fine tool with a wickedly sharp blade.

That first afternoon, no hint of the turbulent Tongariro of two weeks previously remained. A stiff, cold southerly blew. On the way back to the bridge, two querulous paradise ducks flew over, and a big shag, and then, where pine trees and manuka almost meet overhead, whiteheads were suddenly all around, calling cheerily as they clambered in the foliage. They came curiously through the branches to my small whistling sounds. I have never had whiteheads come so close. Two fantails joined them, plainly wondering what all the fuss was about. They flew closer, and perched, posturing, a metre away from me. I kept on whistling, and they began to preen themselves, as though to hide their embarrassment at my improbable birdsong.

Overnight, the southerly blew itself out. Early morning glowed through the window, still, sunny, blue all over. Each of the four mornings opened the same way. I would look out of the bedroom window at green branches frozen against pale blue sky. The whole world out there was utterly still. Yet inside, a shaft of early sunlight thrusting through the kitchen window into the bedroom would illuminate a writhing cavalcade of silver dust motes magically drifting and soaring and circling, in what anyone would otherwise say was absolutely still air.

The third day at the Big O opened with all the early-morning tranquillity of Turangi. So often, strong winds blight fishing days at Otamangakau, sending the fish down, fretting away one's enjoyment of the lake and its austere landscape. But the first hour or so of the third day stayed quite still, while I drifted the Hedgehogger into the lake at the mouth of the inlet canal. No fish came to the fly, but there was entertainment enough in damselflies and paradise ducks. The damselflies were searching for solid perching places, and quickly decided that my person offered welcome opportunities. They drifted to me in twos and threes and fours, some to settle on my hands, and others on my hat. Most were ruby red, but some were blue.

Beyond the canal-mouth in the quiet water to the east, paradise ducks kept up a continual argy-bargy of sound. Only 40 or so were meeting that day, but I have seen five times as many there. Anyone who knows the radio voices of Min, Henry and Bluebottle of *The Goon Show* will laugh at the plaintive conversations of paradise ducks. Petulant little screams from the ducks trigger soothing there-there responses from the drakes. They and the damselflies kept me entertained until the first breezes began to ruffle the lake. I shifted camp to a little bay between McGivern's and Jaws', and caught nothing for hours and hours.

My last day was to treat me no better. My one touch metamorphosed into a rainbow of about half a kilo, which burrowed into a weed-bed, came off, and sent me back a lone green tendril of *Elodea* on the Hedgehogger as a memento of our brief acquaintance.

Otamangakau is like that.

Where they came from

Early angling history is continually unfolding. New information still comes to light to confirm or modify the old. We can only believe what is known at this very moment. It probably won't change, but you never know.

Sometimes a diary from long ago, a chance find in an attic or old newspaper, a name on an ancient greenheart rod, will transform the look of a long-familiar face of history.

Sometimes, painstaking scientific research, which as laymen we know nothing about, will suddenly upend cherished New Zealand angling truths. Unhappily, and just as suddenly, skin-deep research hastily put together for, say, a magazine deadline, will have the same effect. The results of skin-deep research widely communicated are naturally damaging, if not downright damning.

All right, we are not considering the lies that damned the Moriori, only the half-truths and quick stabs at the truth that confuse our understanding of aspects of our angling history. My point, however, is that inaccurate information is so often repeated, time and again, so that, unless it is corrected, it eventually takes on the aura of truth.

Painstaking scientific research unearthed what most people now believe to be the true origins of rainbow trout in New Zealand, but for 54 years prior to 1978 it was believed that steelheads from California's Russian River provided the eggs which founded our rainbow fishery. Unless one or two persistent doubters can prove otherwise, New Zealand's rainbows originated in Sonoma Creek, which admittedly is not too far distant from the Russian River, but far enough to change the history books.

Three shipments of ova from San Francisco arrived for the Auckland Acclimatisation Society in 1883. The first lot, of 10,000, may or may not have been brook trout (the species ordered by the society), but all died en route anyway.

The second and third shipments, comprising 22,000 ova, were more successful, later yielding between 4,000 and 5,000 fish. The society thought they were brook trout (the species ordered), but four years later it correctly identified them as rainbows. In fact, they were steelhead rainbows from Sonoma Creek, but for so many years they were reported to have come from California's Russian River, the source apparently first "authenticated" in 1924 by the then Chief Inspector of Fisheries for the Marine Department, L.F. Ayson, and much later taken up by, for example, O.S.

Hintz in a happy retelling of a Waitahanui rip-fishing episode in his book *Trout at Taupo*.

The true origins were meticulously researched by Dr Donald Scott, of Otago University, and two Californians, J. Hewitson and J.C. Fraser, and published in 1978. Hintz publicly pooh-poohed the trio's *The Origins of Rainbow Trout (Salmo gairdneri Richardson) in New Zealand*. To his credit, however, having been finally convinced of the new truths of the matter, he later equally publicly apologised for his earlier doubts.

Dr Scott also put his considerable talent for research to work on the brown trout that go to sea in the South Island, a subject which had long exercised the minds of trout-fishers, especially that of Canterbury's George Ferris, who, exasperated by the disappearance of local so-called river-dwelling brown trout — presumably out to sea — year after year, concluded that at least a proportion of our earliest stocks of brown trout must have come from a sea trout strain or have later been inadvertently crossed with sea trout.

In the process of researching this problem, Dr Scott went over long-familiar ground in which the original introduction of brown trout was firmly planted. It was essential for him to demonstrate, on the way to possible discoveries of sea trout "interference" with a true strain of brown trout, just how, and from what stocks, the original importations had come about.

According to G.M. Thomson, whose 1922 book, *The Naturalisation of Animals and Plants in New Zealand*, has long made him an authority on the subject, the first attempt to bring brown trout direct to New Zealand was made by A.M. Johnson of Christchurch, "who did actually ship 600 young trout in London in 1864 by the *British Empire*, but a careless deck-hand dropped a lump of white-lead putty into the tank (this was afterwards found at the bottom) and killed all the fish".

Brown trout were successfully introduced for the first time in 1867, when the same A.M. Johnson, as the curator of the Canterbury Acclimatisation Society, brought 800 ova from Tasmania to the society's hatchery in Hagley Park, Christchurch. Only three eggs hatched, and all three fry escaped, but two were later recaptured and luckily proved to be a male and female. Hundreds of waters were stocked with their progeny.

Only recently, a magazine article assuming an authority it did not have, hinted at uncertainties over the origins of the Tasmanian stock from which New Zealand drew its pioneering 800 ova. No mystery surrounds those origins. The story of the introduction of brown trout to Tasmania from England in 1864 is thoroughly documented in *The Acclimatisation of the*

Salmonidae at the Antipodes, by A. Nicols, published in 1882. Nicols and all other authorities affirm that, indeed, the brown trout eggs shipped from London to Tasmania aboard the *Norfolk* came from three south-of-England rivers: tributaries of the Itchen, the Wycombe and the Wey.

According to Donald Scott's paper, *The Migratory Trout (Salmo trutta L.) in New Zealand: I — The Introduction of Stocks*, published in 1964, more importations from the stock in Tasmania were made until at least 1874, but no evidence exists of importations of brown trout direct from Europe until 1883, when one such importation was made. This, incidentally, was the year in which the United States imported its own first brown trout, from Germany. Hence earlier persistent American references to "German browns", a name often used here too.

In his paper, Scott distinguishes between brown trout in coastal waters and true sea trout. He details the introduction of Tweed sea trout to New Zealand from Tasmania and their release in three Otago and Southland rivers between 1872 and 1876. They were progeny of stock which had arrived in Tasmania from Scotland in 1866. Ova from Hodder River sea trout

were also received in New Zealand. They came direct from England in 1868 to Otago, where a few eggs were hatched. Fry were released in the Water of Leith, and possibly also in the Waiwera Stream.

Scott also shows that two shipments of Loch Leven brown trout ova were received by the Otago Acclimatisation Society in 1884, and that some of the ova were left at Wellington. Those two shipments were the first successful ones of Loch Levens to reach New Zealand. All the ova in two earlier shipments, one in 1882 and one in 1883, were dead on arrival, according to Thomson. Such evidence lends no credence to a recent suggestion that Loch Levens were the first, or among the first, brown trout successfully imported into New Zealand.

From the Auckland Acclimatisation Society's own official centenary history, written by C.R. Ashby and published in 1967, it is obvious that the history of brook trout (properly brook char) importations is no more obscure than importations of the more popular species of trout. The Auckland society imported 5,000 American brook trout ova in 1877, of which only 400 were hatched. Ashby says they were liberated in a tributary of the Waikato River near Cambridge, in Lake Pupuke and in the Kaikapakapa Stream. G.M. Thomson, in his book, says that half of the fry were liberated in a tributary of the Waikato near Cambridge, and half in the Kaukapakapa (sic) Stream, Kaipara. Thomson also says that A.M. Johnson of Christchurch also received a considerable stock of eggs in the year that Auckland received theirs.

Thanks largely to the work of Dr Donald Scott and his associates and, before them, to the researches of men like G.M. Thomson, the story of the introduction of each of our major species of trout, and our brook char, is well documented.

One mystery does remain, however; the one surrounding the number, identity, distribution and impact (if any) of possibly two species introduced in 1878 by the Auckland Acclimatisation Society.

According to Ashby, the society imported 30,000 Lake Tahoe trout ova in two shipments that year of 1878, but successfully hatched fewer than 1,000. They were turned out in Lake Waikare, Lake Omapere and the Onehunga Springs, and were never seen again — not surprisingly, in the view of L.F. Ayson, who Thomson quoted in 1922 as saying that no other result could have been expected when such fish were turned out in those waters.

Ayson gave the trout the Latin name of a species of American cutthroat trout. The 1978 Scott, Hewitson and Fraser paper on the rainbow gives the species a different Latin name and calls it the Lahontan cutthroat. Moreover, it quotes different quantities and distribution waters — information obtained direct from the Auckland society's minute-book entries of the time.

Even now, though — unless new evidence has come to light — it is not certain whether the Tahoe trout importations were of cutthroats or of a rainbow trout reputedly native to Lake Tahoe. However, despite the fact that R. Behnke, in a scientific paper he published in 1972, considered that the Lake Tahoe rainbow had not been indigenous to Lake Tahoe after all, Scott, Hewitson and Fraser concluded that, because the identity of the trout in the 1878 introductions was in doubt but was more likely to have been cutthroat, which may have hybridised with later releases of rainbows before, as usual in such cases, losing its identity, "it cannot be maintained that present-day populations of New Zealand rainbow trout are descended from this [1883] shipment only".

Trout Unlimited

I began to think of unlimited trout. Why? Well, trout were decidedly limited where I stood fishing, knee-deep off Lake Taupo's Otuparae Point.

Moreover, heavy rain chirruped and bubbled all around. It had been chirruping and bubbling all around for an hour and a half, right from the moment I had arrived and put the tackle pack down.

Mind you, despite a lack of trout I wasn't abysmally unhappy, not by any means, chiefly because I stayed absolutely warm and dry in the winter downpour. I was snug inside my latest waterproof. This one *is* waterproof, and it *isn't* PVC. At long last, after five so-called waterproofs in about 15 years, this heavy oilskin jacket with the detachable hood fulfils, bless it, the promises of its far-distant makers. None of the others has. Barbour rules!

So I stayed warm and dry in the wet, a condition surely predisposing any angler to philosophical acceptance of a cold and comprehensively rainy day. It helped soften the hardship of no trout, too, although not overmuch.

One or two big shags flew past. I wondered how many illegal trout they had in their possession, packed like sardines in their horrible oily stomachs.

Not many, the freshwater fishery biologists would say, but I know better, don't I?

Slow yachts big and small moved mysteriously here and there in and out of the grey murk between me and Taupo town. Borne on the faint northeasterly wind from behind the town came the flat, staccato, *clap clap* of shotguns. The Taupo Gun Club was hosting the New Zealand Sport Clay Championships. Despite what the fishery biologists say, I could have supplied those shooters with some more exciting and really worthwhile living targets. Mind you, it's the big shags on the little rivers around Taupo that annoy me most.

Still, you can't blame shags for the present shortage of Taupo trout, any more than you can blame any one of many factors influencing the size and availability of the fish population.

Standing there, in the pouring rain, casting and retrieving mechanically, I began to think about unlimited trout again, and then, naturally enough, about Trout Unlimited, the growing movement that complements its longer-established partner in New Zealand, Ducks Unlimited.

Trout Unlimited is much less of a misnomer in New Zealand than it is in the land of its birth, the United States, but misnomer it is if you are logically minded. True, what angler wants to be logical when pollution or destruction of the natural freshwater environment sets emotions alight?

It doesn't matter what lives in the freshwater environment here — trout, eels, salmon, native fish, koura, caddis, nymphs and so on — it's the protection and enhancement, and if necessary rescue, of that environment with which Trout Unlimited is largely concerned.

I think it's a wonderful concept, even though the name only partly describes its intent, which doesn't matter all that much. What really matters is that, steadily growing around New Zealand, is a band of people, most of them trout-fishers, determined to do their bit to protect the sanctity of fresh water and freshwater-fish habitat. They are working to preserve those things and not, as many people suppose from the name, to guarantee New Zealand anglers unlimited trout.

They would never have been able to transform my troutless existence on a wet Sunday afternoon across from Acacia Bay into an afternoon pulsing with tackle-busting lunkers going crazy for the fly. It would have been nice if they had. Even half an hour of unlimited trout would have been thankfully received. But of course the Department of Conservation is the proper overall manager of that particular Taupo scenario, not Trout Unlimited.

Critics scoff and denigrate. Trout Unlimited is America-based, America-inspired, with its chapters and banquets and money-raising auctions. It's a protective organisation designed by and for fishing guides. It's a fishing club, whose members are interested only in preserving the waters in their own back yards. And what's the use of working like slaves to unclog the Hirangi Stream at Turangi, for instance, if poachers now find it all the easier to harvest the subsequent and substantial increase of running fish?

Anyway, say the critics, we already have more than enough fishing clubs and councils, and government departments, and goodness knows what committees, looking after our freshwater fisheries. TU, they say, is like a late spawner digging up a full redd to put down more eggs.

Not so. If there had been no fishing guides and no other vested-interest folk backing the Trout Unlimited movement in New Zealand, the traditional apathy of ordinary anglers — traditional except when faced with issues threatening imminent and devastating repercussions — would probably have brought forth the infant New Zealand Trout Unlimited still-born. As it is, it's alive and well, and starting to kick.

As I see it, three potentially suspect aspects of the movement might cause unease. Any TU-inspired move in New Zealand to promote this country as an exceptionally desirable trout-fishing destination would be seen simply as a device to increase the earnings of its fishing-guide members, and would be totally insupportable. Critics' rejection of the movement on the grounds of guide domination ("It's their livelihood, so let them get on with it, on their own, eh?") would be equally insupportable.

The third aspect concerns all of us: the tendency for fishing guides and tackle-industry people — but particularly guides — to pull against, rather than with, one another, to the detriment of their common aims. How such vested-interest members resolve their differences is entirely their own affair, provided they do it, soon. It maybe hasn't occurred to them often enough or forcibly enough that, in the words of the old adage, unity is strength.

The rain stopped, just like that. I hooked something! I drew a long streamer of *Elodea* or *Lagarosiphon* unresistingly up from the depths just in front of me. That's why I was wading only knee deep. I was perched on the edge of the drop-off where a forest of weed flourishes at the northeastern corner of the Otuparae Point peninsula. I didn't think the weed was welcome there, but it wasn't as unwelcome as the musk weed we fly-fishers had helped first the Wildlife Branch and then DoC to clear from the Whangamata Stream at Kinloch year after year. We had then planted flaxes and native shrubs alongside, to shade the stream and so inhibit any regrowth of musk. Terrible stuff, that musk. Time and again we came across trout helplessly entombed in it.

I thought of the small creek we would soon be working on as members of the newly formed Taupo–Tauhara chapter of Trout Unlimited. We'd sort of get our eye in on that one (it needs spawning-access improvements) before tackling the system of tracks required for another, larger, stream.

Both streams are outside the Taupo Fishing District, so we would be benefiting other anglers, just as one day they would probably benefit us in return.

We would be working in the interests of DoC and the Eastern Region Fish and Game Council. The work is plainly their responsibility, but if they can't discharge that responsibility fully because of lack of funds, then that's where the volunteers come in. That's us, and that's members of fishing clubs too, and anyone else willing to help. Multiply our efforts by the increasing number of freshwater-fishery projects receiving hands-on help from amateurs under the direction of professional conservation staff, and we have a recipe for the enhancement of both freshwater habitat and angling satisfactions.

Furthermore, as Trout Unlimited, we are adding a name to the list of reputable organisations which the politicians, monopolists, bureaucrats and other empire-builders have to reckon with on issues of freshwater-resource protection. Admittedly, individuals can and do exert some influence, but it's the organised groups who carry the real firepower.

Tongariro Walkway

According to the map it's almost 5km along the eastern bank of the Tongariro River from the Red Hut Bridge to the Major Jones Bridge, but, allowing for occasional sidetracking to explore fishing places today, I must have walked 6km from one bridge to the other.

Every step was a delight. It was a beautiful early-autumn day, with the river low and clear, harbouring fish in special places.

A kind friend in Turangi who lives close to the Major Jones Bridge had suggested I leave my car at his home and he would drive me south to the Red Hut Bridge, deposit me there, and look out for me again at his house later in the afternoon.

I had never walked the full distance before, only from the Major Jones Bridge upstream to the tail of the Upper Birch Pool opposite the Tongariro National Trout Centre. Once you have climbed the steps taking you above and beyond the Duchess Pool, you are on a high bank above the river for much of the way to come. Occasional faint tracks lead down to the river between close-growing manuka stems. Not many anglers get this far, or find the tracks, thank goodness, or even bother with the waters they lead to. The crowd prefers the lazy places close to car-parking.

Is it that most anglers are visitors who feel compelled to fill every hour with fishing? I suppose so. Most visitors measure enjoyment only in terms of landed fish. Few prefer exploration and solitude in beautiful surroundings to the hurried compulsion of fish-catching.

Two fish came my way today. The first would definitely have been longer than my middle finger, but only just. The second one was twice as long as the first.

At the head of the Upper Birch, under the canopy of trees there, a trout took something off the surface just as I was about to cast a weighted

Halfback nymph downstream and swing it into the quieter water under the branches. I removed the nymph, tied on a Cicada, and plopped it down 15 metres downstream. Nothing responded, and nothing kept on responding, except that a veritable 2kg rainbow porpoised out from the shaded surface not far from where the first fish had broached, as if to encourage me to continue. So I did. I put on a spindly Brown Spider with partridge hackle — surely the kind of terrestrial that would be falling out of the trees there every five minutes? Nothing agreed with me, several times.

The Tongariro Walkway makes a thoroughly enjoyable walk, whether you're fishing or not. Being a deep orange, my present polaroids accentuate every shade of green, so I walked the track viewing an infinity of cheerful overstatements of that most restful of colours. Fantails greeted me all along the way and responded gratifyingly to my imitations of their calls. Sometimes, swallows flickered along the river, and once a horror-struck heron catapulted off a rock when he caught sight of me.

I startled a young American fly-fisher, too. My greeting spun him round. He hadn't heard me coming. When he told me he had caught one 16cm rainbow, I assured him he had done twice as well as I had; by then I had taken and returned one fish half the size of his.

At the Hydro Pool I came on a barefoot fly-fisher standing on the rock upstream of the junction with the Mangamawhitiwhiti Stream. He waved me airily on my way upstream of the rock.

"Anywhere you like!" he said, but was plainly keeping the anywhere closest to the rock all to himself.

I nymphed slowly up the stretch upstream of the rock. It is ideal nymphing water, and often produces well, but for those very reasons it is of course very well patronised.

Nothing showed any interest at all until I made a last cast and reeled up. Halfway back to me, the fast-moving nymph faltered, and I found myself playing a skittish rainbow no bigger than the span of my spread fingers. It's surprising how strong these little ones are, but of course they quickly come to hand on the tackle you have to use for bigger Tongariro rainbows. This one went back to the river no worse for his brief encounter with the Caddis he so badly wanted.

Thanks, Keith

Keith Gallaugher enjoyed life in Taupo. I believe he enjoyed his last two or three years more than many he had left behind elsewhere. After retirement from a fulfilling and distinguished career in insurance, which took him to various capital cities overseas for varying terms of duty, he detached himself from Auckland to go trout-fishing more often. And who can blame him for that!

Maybe, when he first moved, alone, to Taupo, in the 1980s, he already knew that he would not see out man's normal allotted span of three-score years and ten. He died of cancer towards the end of 1987, leaving behind him in Taupo memories among a great many fly-fishers of an invariably cheerful and extroverted companion who worked tirelessly in the interests of the club he so much enjoyed, the then Taupo Fly-fishers' Club.

He loved cooking. He particulary liked curries of all kinds, and he knew his wine with the intimacy of many years of close and appreciative acquaintance.

He loved classical music. During his last few months in the house he bought to make life more comfortable for himself (rather than continue living in what he called his "little old whare" any longer) he would lie down and immerse himself in the wonder of the music he liked best.

He still went fishing occasionally. A friend or two from the fly-fishers' club would drive him to within a few metres of a Tongariro River pool, and he would fish there happily. When he became too tired to carry on, he would sit on the bank and rest, watching his friends fishing. Latterly, he may not have been able to get to a favourite pool, the one he named the Blackberry Pool, from which he had taken so many good fish in the past.

Also in those closing weeks he was probably no longer tying the trout flies he had been supplying in thousands to a few of the local tackle shops. He had taken up fly-tying gladly, and became adept at it, especially at tying nymphs. He found he had the temperament to tie the same pattern hour after hour, when necessary, to meet his customers' repeat orders.

A member of the family shook her head in disbelief when she knew what he was doing. He didn't think she really understood when he told her what a wonderful thing this fly-tying was for him. He had spent a lifetime in a profession rewarding his intellect. What a change and a joy it was now to work with his hands, and know that he had a ready market for all the flies he cared to make!

He tied a selection of his excellent nymphs for the fly-fishers' clubrooms, and asked me to design a mount and frame them for him. He didn't give me much time, but then his own time was getting desperately short, and he knew it.

Keith put trout-fishing words together as skilfully as trout-fishing nymphs. His feeling for words had unquestionably characterised the many years of his successful career with New Zealand Insurance, but I guess he took a greater pleasure from his fishing words than from his insurance words. And he wanted to be remembered for them.

He had written several short pieces, over the years, for the journal of the Taupo Fly-fishers' Club, and he collected them together and produced a few copies for the club. The thin blue booklet bears no author's name as such, only the pen name he always used, Ikan Tua, a term from his days in Malaysia which he delighted in telling you meant Old Fish.

The story I like best is one he called "Looking Back — And Forward", the one he wrote for the club's 10th anniversary journal, published in August 1985. I am sure he would approve of my introducing it to a much wider audience than it enjoyed at the time, and I do so now, as a tribute to this invariably cheerful man who came to Taupo towards the end of his life and died here too soon.

Old Mr Tau impassively watched the whole process from the bank. He was the station shearer, a proud old Tuhoe who earned my full respect during those long-gone days when school holidays were spent at Rerewhakaaitu.

First there was the long drive from Auckland; then a full hour and a half from Rotorua over the pumice track that left the main road at Rainbow Mountain. There was no electricity; the effects of the great eruption only 50 years previously were still very apparent, but the fishing was good and to an eight-year-old schoolboy it was indeed Paradise.

Father had gone out trolling and I had put up his fly rod and taken it to the lagoon in front of the homestead, and finally managed a cast into the lake. I nearly fell in when a fish took. A bit of a slab it was really, but no fish so proudly shown to a father and no father so pleased with his son's catch.

Old Mr Tau, though, was obviously not impressed, and he said to me after a long period of cogitation that "You pakehas use a lot of fancy gear and spend a lot of time just to catch one plurry slab that's not even good dog tucker, and you come with old Tau tomorrow and I show you how to get the beauties the Maori way, and you bring a sugar bag."

And off we went tomorrow, over the hill to a stream flowing into Rotomahana, loaded up with an empty sugar bag, and home we came a few hours later, sugar bag full and flax stringer loaded with rather large pre-spawned trout. And father, who had had yet another fishless day, he was

pleased not at all, in fact he tried to tell old Mr Tau exactly what he thought of him, but you can't do that successfully to someone who won't listen, can you?

Old Mr Tau, he taught me so much, far more important things than the square root of 144; things like how to see the old matuku pretending he is not there in the raupo; how to call up the fantail; how to appreciate the history of the past; and, yes, how to tickle trout (at least how it used to be done, as I naturally have had no further experience of such goings-on in the past 50 years . . .).

For it was at Rerewhakaaitu at so young an age and so long ago that I caught the trout-fishing disease from which I have never recovered nor for which I have ever had any inclination to take purgative or curative therapy. I have been through its various insidious stages; the primary one of hoping like hell to catch a fish of any size or shape; then the secondary one of wanting to get at least a limit each trip and fertilise the garden accordingly; the tertiary or snobbish stage where the best trophy, naturally on the dry fly, was the compulsion; and then latterly the terminal stage where I go fishing when and where the mood dictates, when I kill the occasional prime fish for the table, but often get nothing, always having, though, a great day's fishing.

This terminal stage has only really hit me since I bought my Taupo whare (for reasons not related to fishing at all). It didn't take long for the disease to erupt, although initially I found the Taupo virus a little — no, let's be honest, vastly — different from the small-stream, dry-fly, brown-trout strain that I had mainly enjoyed prior to retirement.

But I'm now irrevocably under the magic spell of the Taupo area, where I quickly found that I could practise any type of angling I wanted on any particular day within easy driving distance; whether throwing a Woodsie Bomb into the Tongariro, a Kemsley Marabou into the lake, or a Dad's Favourite dry into a bush stream. It's all there for us to enjoy, and it's not far away. We've got it made!

I joined the club, now celebrating its 10th anniversary, and it has been a privilege to have attended fairly regularly the enjoyable Friday night meetings. I enjoy the fellowship, the guests who turn up from all parts of the world, the occasional trips to the river with a fellow-member, the swapping of home-tied nymphs and flies, the sharing of secret possies. I have enjoyed my four years to date, and am sorry at having missed the previous six.

I also enjoy writing the occasional not-too-serious little yarn for the club magazine.

But this article is for the anniversary edition, and so is very much of a more serious nature. Perhaps I can then finally get to my plea. Let's all enjoy the club and the great facilities it offers; let's all support it to the full; let's all support the committee in its management and also in its untiring efforts to present our views in trying to preserve our relatively unspoiled rivers and lakes and countryside, and above all our beloved sport of trout-fishing, so that all may still be available to our children's children.

Let us all vigorously assist in enforcing this preservation on the bureaucrats, the despoilers, the self-interested piscatorial assassins, and the polluters.

Incidentally, have you ever seen a dying blue heron still frantically trying to disentangle itself from a bunch of discarded nylon? Are you one of those who continually throw unwanted lengths of the stuff on the riverbank?

I can't pick it all up, you know. I would need a plurry sugar bag each trip. Sugar bag? Ah yes; thanks, old Mr Tau.

Boatman on the table

Sitting in the study with the lights on during midsummer evenings, I am aware of all manner of moths and midges. On warm, still nights the insects swarm to the big windows overlooking the lake. If the weather stays humid, and if the curtains aren't drawn across the windows, extraordinary numbers of insects flock to the glass. Over the past two nights, scores of large, dark brown moths have appeared. Some have found their way into the house, and I have removed a dozen or so. I cannot remember ever having seen them before, but many different species come to the windows and perhaps this particular one has not hitherto been present in such numbers in the neighbourhood.

Tonight, checking manuscript proofs, I gradually became aware of a chunky fly about a centimetre long on the big table I use as a desk. It was trapped in the open mouth of a folded clear-plastic bag.

After a while, seeing movement there again, I took a closer look, wondering why the fly hadn't flown or crawled away. It appeared to be skidding around on the plastic. And that is exactly what it was doing, but it was rowing rather than skidding, rowing with the little oars of the water boatman.

The night was stiflingly warm and humid. Possibly it was the perfect night for a water boatman to fly away from home and seek its fortune. I had never encountered one in the open air before, although it is well known that the water boatman is not solely an aquatic insect.

Well, I winkled him out of his clear-plastic skating rink, took him outside and consigned him to the night.

Afterwards, I was sorry. I ought to have taken a torch and gone down to the birdbath and consigned him to that, to find out whether he was indeed a gentlemanly water boatman, which always swims right way up, or the water boatman's villainous lookalike, the back-swimmer, which, as its name suggests, rows along on its back.

Bob Bragg, angler

If you come across an old fly-fisherman somewhere in the South Island intently pursuing the gentle art from a VW campervan headquarters, it will almost certainly be Bob Bragg, of Christchurch.

You will be lucky to have found him though. Bob's greatest joy is fishing alone well off the beaten track. He loves getting into the back country, where his fine trout flies account for scores of browns and rainbows every season.

Bob Bragg has tied flies all his life. Ever since his schooldays at Sedbergh, Yorkshire, in the early 1930s, he has tied flies and fished for trout and salmon; and he still does, bringing a lifetime of knowledge and experience, and a burning enthusiasm unquenched by the passing years, to the sport he loves.

He would be the envy of many anglers — a man whom fishing has enchanted as a career and as a sport. Many anglers reject the notion of happiness in angling as a career. Bob values his fly-fishing leisure more than most, and ever since he began helping in Thomas Greenbank's Sedbergh tackle shop more than 60 years ago and learnt to tie local hackle flies there, he has been happy in the trade of sport-fishing, too.

From Sedbergh he went to Hutchinson's of Kendal, hook-makers and sellers of fishing tackle, and then south to London, where he worked first in Cogswell and Harrison's gunsmithing and fishing-tackle shop in Piccadilly, and then in Ogden-Smith's, not far away at 62 St James's Street, where incidentally he met the great G.E.M. Skues himself (who wasn't impressed with the shop's nymphs).

In April 1939, he signed an agreement which was to take him to the kind of fishing he had dreamt of, the kind his father had experienced on a tour of New Zealand just after the turn of the century. Tisdall's of Christchurch wanted Bob Bragg to work for them, but first they wanted him to write a report on the British fishing-tackle trade of 1934–1939.

He arrived in Christchurch the day before the new trout-fishing season of 1939 opened, and on November 5 he caught a Selwyn River trout above Whitecliffs. In 1989 he celebrated his golden jubilee of angling in New

Zealand, on November 5, by catching a trout in the same place.

His arrival in Christchurch began a 36-year association with the city's fishing-tackle trade, and a love affair with New Zealand trout and salmon fishing which is now into its 55th year.

Across that span of years, memorable Bragg catches include three Young River rainbows averaging 3.4kg taken on Bluebottle and Irresistible dry flies; 24 Tauranga–Taupo River rainbows averaging 2.2kg taken on a nine-day April camping holiday; and, most noteworthy of all, a bag of 14 Rakaia River salmon averaging 5.2kg taken in 7¾ hours of fishing some 8km up from the rivermouth.

That day of the salmon, Bob was on leave from the Royal New Zealand Navy, with which he served almost five years. After his discharge in 1946, he resumed his old job with Tisdall's in Christchurch for three years, then worked for himself at home for five years, tying flies and making "Wairarapa" split-cane rods. Then followed a further eight years with Tisdall's up to 1962, followed in turn by 13 years working for himself again (tying and selling "Wairarapa" flies), and others in the trade.

He concluded his working life, at Briscoe's, on his 60th birthday, and later wrote thankfully that on that day, 6 January 1975, he retired from the city and went fishing.

Bob started a fishing diary in 1932, and in 1990 it was still going strong. One hopes that some time in the future it will be presented to the Canterbury Public Library and preserved there for all time.

Hopefully it will be joined by two books which Bob Bragg has assembled over the past three years. They embody hundreds of clippings, illustrations, diary notes and articles about fishing. The first one is called *An Introduction to Fishing in the British Isles and Overseas, 1915–1939.* Besides the original, only three photocopies exist. One of them is lodged with the Flyfishers' Club of London.

Bob plans to make six copies of his second book, a similarly kaleidoscopic mixture of notes, jottings, pictures and magazine and newspaper clippings. It will record the 50 years of freshwater sport-fishing in the South Island between 1940 and 1990.

Both books, says Bob, are the outcome of a decision to make use of the voluminous fishing records he has amassed during the 60 years of his passionate interest in angling.

Without these books, Britain's and New Zealand's angling history would be the poorer. Nowhere else could one find, collected together, the personal and practical experiences of scores of accomplished anglers in Britain and New Zealand, and elsewhere, during the years covered.

Bob Bragg's angling memorabilia, complemented by his own fly-fishing and fly-tying knowledge, have served other valuable purposes, notably in Keith Draper's book *Trout Flies in New Zealand*, in which many patterns and observations are sourced to the Christchurch fly-tier.

Never a man to withhold information, Bob has often spent hours in research for others, painstakingly finding and listing fishing and fly-tying references likely to help his correspondents. He is equally helpful dispensing the fruits of his fly-fishing successes.

For instance, although he once favoured just four patterns of fly for back-country rainbows — Alder, Cridge's Terror, Grey Sedge and Greenwell — he now advocates Black Gnat, Waitaki Sedge and March Brown variant nymphs. He says he gets a good response to these nymphs in broken water, and fished downstream on occasion, too.

In a recent December he fished sedge on the upper Waitaki, and found that both rainbows and browns would take between 8.00am and 10.00am as readily as in the evening. He caught his fish on a quartet of special flies, all tied on long-shanked hooks, sizes 12–14: a Gowan Nymph, a Gavin Olive Nymph, a Waitaki Sedge Pupa, and a Waitaki Sedge for surface feeders.

Caddis (sedge) should really loom larger in fly-fishers' minds and fly boxes than they do now, he feels, because judged by the behaviour and stomach contents of trout in both lakes and rivers, the *Trichoptera* are a favourite, sought-after food at all stages.

His continual searching, experimenting and recording will hopefully encourage Bob Bragg to write a book of his own one day, distilling the best of his and others' angling experience. Just now, coming to an end of his second very substantial compilation of memorabilia, his thoughts are no doubt turning from a half-century of South Island sport-fishing to another project dear to his heart — a new approach to imitating, with a minimum of "pattern", a range of aquatic insects taken by trout.

In common with so many anglers who thoroughly enjoy their sport, Bob knows that there is far more to angling than merely catching fish. He loves the world of nature surrounding the waters in which he is privileged to fish, and he loves all the other peripheral delights, of tackle, natural and artificial flies, conversation over convivial ales, books, and endless conjecture and experiment.

May those simple things long continue to captivate the heart and mind of Bob Bragg, of Christchurch.

It's De Lautour at last!

After winning a battle with solicitors acting for a Japanese company buying up yet another piece of New Zealand, my win against some Wellington bureaucrats over the correct name for a pool and a reach on two world-famous New Zealand trout streams seems very small beer indeed.

Mind you, it wasn't a total win. It would have been total if I were a product of our present educational system; but my continuing membership of the Apostrophic Church, and all that that implies, robbed my victory of some of its satisfactions.

Apostrophic Church? Well, that's the pre-1970s or thereabouts movement that our English teachers of those days coolly suppressed. They didn't want to know about apostrophes, so they didn't want the children to know about apostrophes either. Some of those children have in their turn become teachers, and so the denial of apostrophic wisdom goes on — and on. Apostrophes have suffered an eclipse. Genocide would be a better word.

Happily, the Apostrophic Church thrives overseas. The United States is a particular champion of the Apostrophic Church. Even flourishing American fishing magazines take pride in their apostrophes, and all in the right places too. Millions upon millions of apostrophes have found refuge in the United States and other English-writing countries. Here in New Zealand, apostrophes have long gone into the too-hard basket.

Sorry, I get a bit hot under the collar over the absence or misuse of the apostrophe in New Zealand, especially the possessive apostrophe, the one signifying ownership or close association with something; such as Rewi's Last Stand, Murray's Mistake, Parsons' Glory, De Lautour's Pool.

Ah yes, De Lautour's Pool. I have been wandering from the point.

De Lautour's Pool will sadly become De Lautours Pool in future on certain maps of the Taupo district published by the Department of Survey and Land Information. But at least, and at last, they've got the spelling of the name right: De Lautour, not Delatour.

However, like so many people and organisations the length and breadth of New Zealand, the department has incarcerated untold numbers of apostrophes. Even its cartographers don't want a bar of apostrophes. They make too much "noise" on their maps, so they tell me; and they take up too much room on maps crowded with names.

Maybe we could sell off our huge surplus of apostrophes to the big apostrophe-friendly world overseas for a dollar a throw and halve the national debt?

Anyway, the satisfaction of at long last winning official approval for De Lautour and the dropping of Delatour is not too greatly diminished by the department's intransigence over apostrophes.

By the merest chance I saw a New Zealand Geographic Board advertisement in the local paper. It announced an Intention to Assign Place Names, and the place names were the names of all the Tauranga–Taupo and Waitahanui fishing pools. Apparently they all needed legitimising. Apart from the seriously inconsistent use of apostrophes, I saw at once that they'd got De Lautour spelt wrongly, again — an error to which I had drawn attention as long ago as 1973. The board called for objections to the names, so I objected, and backed up my particular objection with some of the interesting story of Ernest de Lautour in New Zealand, many years ago.

Ernest de Lautour fished certain places on the Tongariro River, and the Waitahanui River, around the turn of the century, as often and as success-fully as Major Jones of the Tongariro and Gordon Williams of the Waitahanui later fished theirs. After a time in Tokaanu, Ernest lived on the Waitahanui River for seven years in a tiny cottage, and apparently paid the Maori landowners two bags of flour a year for the privilege.

He was a fanatical fisherman, and in 1904 was secretly catching huge rainbow trout in the Waitahanui. A.H. Chaytor, visiting de Lautour in 1917, assumed him to be Irish, but we now know that he was born in Hexton, England. Ever since his long association with the Waitahanui, the pool immediately upstream of the state highway bridge at Waitahanui has been known as Delatour's.

Ernest came to New Zealand from fisheries work in South Africa. He was known to be fishing the Tongariro in 1898 for the big browns in the river, and then the Waitahanui in 1904 for both browns and rainbows, having exchanged his thatched hut south of the lake for a similar one further north. Malcolm and Forrestina Ross, the couple responsible for releasing the first rainbows into upper Waikato River headwaters in 1898, on behalf of the Wellington Acclimatisation Society, considered de Lautour to have been "the pioneer fisherman, almost, of the Tongariro".

Undoubtedly he qualified equally as an original on the Waitahanui: his name would not otherwise be honoured on both rivers.

Despite his presumably successful fisheries work in South Africa, where, for instance, he is credited with hatching the first trout liberated in the Cape Colony, de Lautour's fisheries management appointments in New Zealand were short-lived.

Strangely, too, this lonely, chronically asthmatic angler, who was said to have come to New Zealand from South Africa to manage the Welling-ton Acclimatisation Society's Masterton Hatchery, is also said to have been brought out from London for the job: a sum of £36 10s ($73.00) for the cost of his passage and etceteras from England to Wellington appears in the Wellington society's records.

Oddly, too, although the year of de Lautour's death, 1918, seems defi-nite enough, only his death certificate will settle the puzzle of where he died.

The English barrister A.H. Chaytor, himself a noted angler and author of that salmon-fishing classic *Letters to a Salmon Fisher's Sons*, visited Taupo in 1917, staying at the Terraces Hotel (now De Brett Thermal Hotel) half a mile from de Lautour's "tiny wooden cot of one room", to which he had moved from his reed hut on the Waitahanui. In his second book, *Essays Sporting and Serious*, Chaytor talks of de Lautour and his conversations with him, and then says that the man died the year following his visit. To me, Chaytor makes it sound as though de Lautour died in Taupo. Indeed, the English periodical *Fishing Gazette*, to which de Lautour contributed articles, reported in its August 24 issue of 1918 that de Lautour's copy of that issue had been returned from Taupo bearing the postmark "Deceased". Yet a distant cousin in New Zealand, writing about Ernest's later years, reported that he had died destitute in the Hitchin Infirmary, England. No date was given.

Chaytor's reference in his second book kindled my interest in de Lautour. At last the name of that Waitahanui River pool was explained. But why was it spelt Delatour's Pool?

Eighteen years ago I first wrote that it would be nice to put the record straight. Three years later, in 1976, the matter was made more widely public in a book of mine, *Parsons' Glory*. I am glad that at last the record is being put straight, and all because I happened to see an advertisement in the local paper.

One day, when hopefully New Zealand resumes diplomatic and educational relations with the Apostrophic Church, we shall be able to put the record even straighter.

Hedgehoggers revealed

Very little is new under the fly-tying sun. Some years ago I could find no reference in fly-tying books old or new to a method of skirting lures with fur which had suddenly been developed by a local fly-tier. The man and his method plainly deserved the warmest praise, and they got it.

It was only a year or two later, reading J.C. Mottram's *Fly-fishing: Some New Arts and Mysteries*, that I found the method described in detail there — a revelation published 60 years before the Taupo fly-tier "invented" the very same method.

Now the same thing has happened again. This time, though, the so-called innovation concerns not a method but a fly-tying material. Both Gil Brandeis and I had never heard or read of the material being used for fly-dressing. No-one else claimed any knowledge of it either. Quite simply, then, it seemed as though Gil should be congratulated as the first fly-tier ever to use the material. But I ought to have known better.

Congratulations were certainly in order. Even before Gil could try out for himself a fly tied with the new fibres, I had hooked two fish within 10 minutes of the start of a first trial of the pattern. That day, my only regret was that Gil himself hadn't yet had a chance to fish the new fly.

A few weeks later I twice tested the pattern at Lake Otamangakau. Four fish took a fancy to it, three of them within two hours on the first occasion, and one on the last.

Now if that isn't fast work for The Big O I don't know what is, outside of the frenzied days of the annual cicada carnival there. Two of the first three fish let go, but the third hung on until I released her a few minutes later, a fine rainbow of around 4kg.

As a reminder, however, that one must take the fishing rough with the fishing smooth, especially at Lake Otamangakau, I have to say that the gods decreed that I should fish there two days later for four hours and record just one early attack on Gil's fly, an attack which metamorphosed into a bustling little rainbow of half a kilo which rocketed into the air time and again before I could land it and set it free.

I don't know what the six trout — two in running water and four in still — took the fly for. Because of its shaggy appearance they could have taken it for a washed-under emerger, or a hatching pupa; or perhaps a female fly of a species which climbs down below the surface to deposit eggs.

The egg-laying-female possibility seems likely in the case of the river trout. I had tied on the new fly as a dropper above a slim but heavy caddis tail fly, and both trout took the dropper literally on the drop.

We called it a Hedgehogger: hardly an imaginative name — not like Jersey Herd, or Thunder and Lightning — but Gil was quite happy with it. The fly doesn't roll up into a ball when attacked by a trout, nor is it covered in prickles, although it does feel faintly prickly to the touch, like fine, stiff straw. And that is not altogether surprising to anyone who knows the texture of hedgehog fur, for hedgehog fur is the material Gil has used for this initially highly successful fly.

Except for a single small partridge hackle to represent legs, the fly is all hedgehog fur. We thought it all new, too, until, only two weeks after I had planned an accolade for Gil's inventiveness, I happened to read Arthur Ransome's book *Mainly about Fishing*, in which he devotes a chapter to an eighteenth-century English poacher's book, *The North Country Angler*, published, if you please, in 1786. The anonymous author gives a dressing for the green drake (mayfly), which incorporates a dubbed body of "camel or bear's hair or urchin's [hedgehog's] belly ribbed yellow silk with green wax . . ."

If that isn't enough, I have just found two references to hedgehog fur in a book I have waited years to read — Ian Niall's *Trout from the Hills*, published in 1961. He suggests hackling a Coch y Bonddu wet fly with starling feathers, or furs, bristle or the hair from a hedgehog. Later, recalling his difficulty in trying to duplicate some Canadian deer-hair flies, he said a friend in Ireland came to his rescue with a fly made from the belly hair of a hedgehog and a hackle at front and rear. Deer-hair flies are meant to float though, whereas hedgehog fur sinks, so I guess Ian Niall's search did not end with his friend's letter from Ireland.

Gil ties his pattern on a Mustad 94840 size 12 hook, using a waxed brown tying silk, eight turns of fine lead wire, three of the coarsest straight hedgehog hairs for the tail, a dubbed body ribbed with fine gold wire, and a single turn of partridge hackle behind the head sloping backwards.

He recommends dubbing the fly using the tying-thread-loop method detailed in many fly-tying books. Wax the loop of pre-waxed silk before

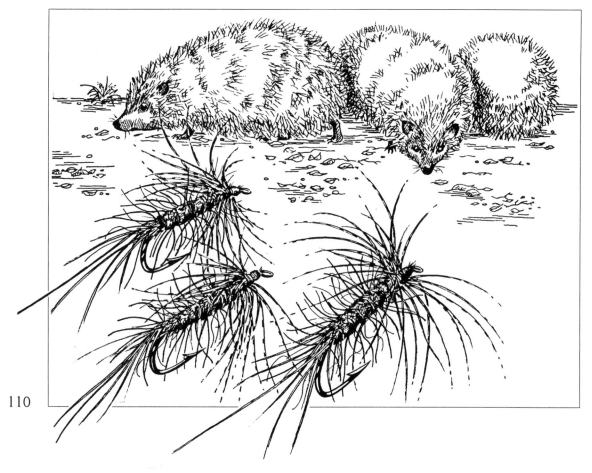

spreading a pinch of fur up the loop and then securing the trapped fibres by twisting the loop tight. Then wind the "rope" up the body. Wind the gold-wire ribbing the other way up the body. Tease out trapped fibres with a needle, and cut off any unnaturally long fibres. But, says Gil, in trimming, don't detract from the fly's rough appearance.

Pondering the matter of Gil's Hedgehoggers and the success of my first trials with them, I fleetingly imagined thousands of kilometres of New Zealand roads relieved of their traditional toll of hedgehogs as fly-tying anglers carried out dawn swoops, thus possibly conferring endangered-species status on our scavenger of the roads, the harrier.

Gil found his initial supply of material floating in his goldfish pond attached to one very dead hedgehog. By that time, presumably, all the fleas had abandoned ship.

That's something to remember about hedgehog fur: make sure the donors are well and truly cold before you get busy with the scissors.

Our first book of trout-fishing

Poor Spackman. Imagine being confined to bed, helpless with rheumatic paralysis, for two and a half years, and then dying at age 46 while your wife and the two younger children, aboard the steamship *Tongariro*, outward bound from England, are still three weeks away from your bedside.

This was the man who, a little over 100 years ago, in 1892, wrote New Zealand's very first book of trout-fishing. He called it *Trout in New Zealand: Where to Go and How to Catch Them*. It is a little book of 100 pages, bound in blue cloth, with gold-blocked title and author's name on the cover.

The copy I unearthed in Smith's bookshop in Wellington's Mercer Street in 1965 cost me 7s 6d (75c). A rare mint-condition copy, with the folding plan of the Masterton Hatchery, and the folding map of the North Island and "Middle Island" trout streams, without tear or blemish, might fetch as much as $350.00 these days.

The title page tells us that W.H. Spackman, B.A., Barrister at Law, was the President of the Canterbury Anglers' Society and Counsel to the Canterbury Acclimatisation Society. Strangely, the book was published by authority of George Didsbury, the Government Printer. That made it a government publication. Why should the government publish New Zealand's first book of trout-fishing?

Spackman's obituary in *The Press*, Christchurch, tells us that he was an acknowledged authority on fishing matters, and wrote the book for the government. The Liberal Government of those days was apparently anxious to promote New Zealand's scenic and sporting attractions. They knew that this well-respected and public-spirited barrister and solicitor of Christchurch had published articles in the English *Field* magazine encouraging fishermen to come to New Zealand. He was obviously just the man to write a comprehensive official handbook and guide which would hopefully attract increasing numbers of anglers to the excellent fishing to be had in the colony.

By the cruellest of ironies, this devoted trout-fisher died on the opening day of the Canterbury trout-fishing season of 1896. Had he been quite well, he would undoubtedly have fished that day with his close friends A.M. Ollivier and A.H. Marciel. Perhaps the three of them would have slept the previous night at the Selwyn Huts, all ready for the morning. In 1888 they had pooled resources and built a crib there, at the mouth of the Selwyn. It was a favourite river. One day the following year, 1889, Spackman landed probably his best bag of trout from the river, 14 of them, weighing 71lb (32.25kg). Some of them might well have been the progeny of the 2,000 fish liberated some years earlier by the founder of the well-known Christchurch law firm of the time, W.H. Wynn-Williams, with whom Spackman worked before starting out on his own.

That same year of 1889, as president of the Canterbury Anglers' Society, Spackman wrote to the Commissioner of Crown Lands asking that a strip of land along the bank of the Selwyn near the mouth of the river be set aside as an angling reserve. Fishermen, he wrote, had need of a fenced area there in which to tether their horses.

Land was formally set aside, and in 1896 the commissioner asked the anglers' society to nominate three of its members to serve on what was to become the Selwyn Domain Board. Had he lived, Spackman would have welcomed the chance to serve on that board, but he never saw the fenced area he had asked for — or the trees, to the value of £5.0s 0d ($10.00), voted by the domain board for the angling reserve.

He knew the Selwyn, and all the other rivers of Canterbury, intimately; so intimately, in fact, that he needed no-one else to help him describe them for his book, or to tell readers where to find them, how they were stocked by the settlers, and how to catch the trout in them. But he had help from angling friends and acclimatisation societies outside Canterbury for the rest of the book.

Reading it, you might think that his North Island sources must have been models of brevity. The island's trout-fishing merits a mere nine pages. By contrast, the South Island receives 50 pages. Of course the rainbow trout, which was to transform the North Island's fisheries, had only been introduced into Auckland, as ova from California, nine years earlier. The great rainbow fishery in the north was only in its infancy. In the south, the brown trout was firmly entrenched, although why Spackman appeared to favour Otago's claim to the initial successful introduction of brown trout rather than that of Christchurch, his adopted city, remains something of a mystery.

Those were great days in the south! By our standards, more than 100 years on, trout were enormous, and enormously prolific. They were caught on bullies, spinners and cicadas, and on grasshoppers, biggish wet flies and creepers. The creeper, said Spackman, was the finest possible lure for trout. In those days, trout taken on the fly seldom exceeded 2.2kg. If you wanted really big fish, bullies or other small fish were the answer. Up to 1892, the largest trout caught on rod and line weighed 12kg. It was taken out of Hall's Creek on livebait by Mr Lambie of Leeston.

The serious fisherman was obliged to use a very powerful rod if he wanted to avoid breakages. Spackman warned that common English fly-rods were of very little use; they were never made to hold New Zealand trout. Luckily, however, the makers at Home now knew what was required. Messrs Hardy Bros of Alnwick were making a special New Zealand rod.

At long last, then, the colonists' stories of huge trout were being believed. Hitherto, said Spackman, it was not too much to say that no New Zealand angler had dared to speak the truth at Home for fear of being looked upon as an unmitigated "something", and many a colonist could look back with pain on the polite silence with which his perfectly truthful statements had been met in many a London club.

Perhaps Spackman had told his own perfectly truthful stories in London clubs and had had them greeted with the same polite silence? That's assuming that he made the voyage home now and again between the year he arrived in Christchurch from England, 1879, and 1893, the year his illness forced him to retire from active business and community life.

Both he and his wife were English. He was born in Westwood, and she was from Orpington. He may well have talked overenthusiastically of the trout-fishing to be had in New Zealand, and been politely disbelieved by his listeners.

He would have been glad to get back to Christchurch, both to his legal practice and to the very real big trout of the province. He would have been glad to immerse himself once more in all the activities and interests that, as a professional man, and a man of means, he obviously found time for.

His first 12 years in Christchurch would have been the happy and rewarding ones that any man enthused by fishing and acclimatisation would have experienced.

History reminds us, though, that Spackman had more weighty responsibilities at various times during those 12 years. He was a member of the Board of Governors of Canterbury College, took an active interest in the Public Library, was at one time the New Zealand Commissioner for Lunatic Asylums, became the Canterbury District Law Society's Standing Counsel, a provisional director of the New Zealand Boot and Shoe Company, and chairman of the board of the ill-fated New Zealand Southern Cross Petroleum Company.

On the lighter side, he succeeded Mr R.W. Fereday in 1885 as captain of the local archery club.

The Press obituary mentions what was possibly the one bright spot in Spackman's last year or so of life. He had a little flutter on the Melbourne Cup, and won himself £13,500 ($27,000), a small fortune in those days. But fancy winning that amount of money and not being able to celebrate the occasion . . .

So crippling was his paralysis that he was unable even to sign his will or two of its three codicils. He was just able to sign the third codicil, at a time when, as his obituary put it, "Mr Spackman still had good hopes . . . of recovering." But it was not to be. His condition deteriorated. No doubt an urgent cable was despatched to Mrs Spackman in England, who hurriedly took ship with two of the children back to New Zealand. But too late. Poor Spackman.

Trout *quintet*

They say the late Jack Thorburn built the first motel complex in New Zealand. He built it at Motuoapa, Lake Taupo; and as far as I know he built it some time in the 1950s.

The fourth time I stayed there, in the early 1960s, was with George. We were on our way home to Wellington after helping to put up a huge stand for our company, BP, at the Easter Show in Auckland.

Back in head office later I was hauled over the coals for my audacity. Who did I think I was, the managing director or something, to break a journey from Auckland to Wellington and stay the night?

It was no accident that I broke the journey at Motuoapa. There was trout-fishing gear in the boot of the company car. Mine, of course, for George was no fisherman. His particular passions were photography, film-club activity and music. What he didn't know about classical music wasn't worth knowing.

We cooked ourselves a meal that night at the motel, then I took George on a fishing trip after dark to the mouth of the Waimarino River. As we made our way along the track by torchlight I began whistling a happy tune. No wonder! This was a lot better than working in Auckland, or motoring back overnight to Wellington.

George asked, curiously, whether I knew what I was whistling, and I said I didn't have the faintest idea. And that was quite true. It was just another tune I knew and sometimes whistled.

"It's called the *Trout*," said George.

"Nonsense," I said.

"True," said George. "It comes from the fourth movement of Schubert's *Trout* quintet."

What an extraordinary coincidence! Of the thousands of tunes I knew and whistled, usually utterly oblivious of their names and origins, I had tonight chosen one called "The Trout" and was whistling it in the company of a man who could identify it — on our way to catch trout!

But that was the only trout I "played" that night.

A few years later, in 1969, five of the world's most talented young musicians came together to rehearse the *Trout* quintet and finally give a performance at the then new Queen Elizabeth Hall in London, on 30 August of that same year.

If you attended that performance, or have seen the film that was made of it and the rehearsals beforehand, and the offstage delight of the performers in their music, and their friendship one with the other, you would feel as so many have since felt about that exuberant group and its remarkable collective talent.

Perhaps, like me, you take no great interest in classical music except when some melody you know and like emerges suddenly from a performance and briefly lights up, for you, an otherwise dimly lit occasion.

Even the other movements of the *Trout* quintet now have significance for me. The fourth movement and its recurring, lilting melody, is plainly more appealing than the others, which lack memorable tunefulness. But now that, by way of the modern miracle of video-coupled television, I can command a performance at any time, my aural appreciation of the film grows and grows.

Television has introduced classical music and instrumentalists to an immense audience. Just now, the Pavarottis and the Dame Kiris of this world hold sway. But a little over 20 years ago, the people who performed the *Trout* quintet that August night in London were the darlings of the European and American worlds of classical music. Their names won't live as long as Schubert's will. Naturally enough, instrumentalists, however profoundly talented, hardly ever endure as long in public esteem as composers.

But our five of the quintet that memorable night of 1969 will nevertheless live long in the appreciation and affection of millions. Especially will the name of the young English woman Jacqueline du Pré endure as one of the world's greatest virtuosi of the cello; and as a martyr to the multiple sclerosis which ended her life so tragically early.

The other four musicians that memorable evening in the Queen Elizabeth Hall were Jacqueline du Pré's husband Daniel Barenboim, Itzhak Perlman, Pinchas Zukerman and Zubin Mehta. I, for one, am very glad they honoured Schubert with that performance, for they also honoured, by implication, the trout, and trout-fishers, too. We can forgive them the little touches of humour that enlivened the players from time to time, humour that perhaps may not have surfaced had Schubert called his piece of music, say, "Voices of the Brook". Their little secretive smiles seemed to say "Fancy performing a piece of music about a fish — but isn't it fun!"

T.C. Kingsmill Moore, the distinguished Irish fly-fisher and Supreme Court judge who gave us that excellent book *A Man May Fish*, believed that it was a little hill-stream trout, in its "livery of saffron and umber with garnet buttons down the sides" that made the model for Schubert's quintet. "Surely it was a piece of impudence no longer than his hand that Schubert has sent lilting down the centuries!" he observes.

Mr Justice Kingsmill Moore wrote his book almost a decade before the 1969 performance of the *Trout* quintet in London. I like to think that he heard that talented quintet of young players that night; or, if not then, perhaps later, for according to another fisherman and writer, Logie Bruce Lockhart, those particular players transformed the vulgarity of incurably

English performers, who did the piece to death, into virtual perfection. Says Mr Lockhart, in his book *The Pleasures of Fishing*:

> It is pure, sunlit, water music; the essence of spring by the brookside. The phrases dart and trill, ebb and flow in interweaving liquid patterns: they are like eddies and swirls and bubbles, sparkling and dazzling their rhythmic way over a gleaming mosaic of pebbles. The cameras did it all justice: hands and arms, smiling lips, and raised eyebrows, bows and keys performed a ballet: melodies and accompaniments shuttled back and forth as faces were utterly lost in the joy of recreation.

I'm not one for watching television or listening to chamber music, but from time to time I play that video film of ours and sit there enthralled as those five young musicians once again bring a trout to life within "eddies and swirls and bubbles . . . over a gleaming mosaic of pebbles".

Scuttling to an assignation

Someone had dropped a walnut-sized bunch of fluorescent red yarn on the beach close to where the little Mapara Stream rushes helter-skelter out of green-leafed obscurity, and dashes, four big strides of it, to the lake. You get your feet wet if you walk across, but sometimes you can jump it dry.

That red yarn was a long way from home, home being the meeting of a fly-line and leader fishing the upstream nymph on any fishable Taupo river. Any fishable Taupo river was certainly not the little Mapara Stream, which, aside from poachers, enjoys the sanctity of spawning water.

Even as I bent down to pick up the nympher's strike indicator, the hurrying chuckle of the stream changed key. I couldn't believe my eyes. A deep-bodied rainbow trout of a kilo and a half was scuttling for its life up the beach. Half out of the water, spray flying from frenzied fins, the fish scurried between the rocks and into the green sanctuary above.

Well, I had come quietly to the stream on my way back to the car from two hours of casting practice. Yes, the day was overcast, and yes, light rain had begun to fall as I came to the stream. But at half past three in the afternoon you don't expect a rainbow trout to go surfing across the Whakaipo beach in front of you to keep a spawning appointment somewhere upstream.

Half past three in the morning, in decent darkness, yes; but not on a

bright and dreamy afternoon, with the broken willows' autumn crowns the colour of claret, and last week's storm-tossed weed-banks whitening on the shore, and the water quite like a mirror all around, and the five resident swans alternately upending and listening, puzzled, to the paradise ducks' outcry.

I am not a duck-shooter; but I could have done with a mate with a shotgun that afternoon, to make an end of the ducks' mindless cacophony, too close. The drakes might not have thanked me for ridding them of their lifetime partners' petulant screams, but I wouldn't have been unduly worried. I did throw stones at one of the ducks, which would have been well within range of my stone-throwing arm of 1943; but 50 years later, stone-throwing distance had sadly diminished.

That infuriating paradise duck only paddled further out of range before doubling the intensity and frequency of her hysteria.

Perhaps the first week of May traditionally sets sheldrake and shelduck passions alight? My end of Whakaipo Bay, so dreamily peaceful to start with, became a riot of screaming and honking and posturing paradise pairs stamping their authority on this and that bit of water.

Their relentless shrieks and skirmishes hardly helped cushion my failure to hook a fish, and by quarter past three I had had enough. Once or twice a westerly breeze had faintly blown, but for the most part the lake resembled only infinitesimally animated pewter. Such metallic calm rarely breeds daylight-fishing success at Whakaipo. True, three fish broached, and a kingfisher rocketed past to a willow, and shags hung out their wings, but never a fish touched a fly of mine repeatedly hunting far and wide.

This was the third time in two weeks that I had gone to Whakaipo and drawn a blank. The first time, the sun shone bravely, but a fierce, wild wind whipped up waves as big as the ocean-going variety and drove them thunderously along the beach. I fished the comparatively sheltered reach, but the wind and the waves and the pea-soup thickening perceptibly as the southwesterly freed and served up all manner of weed flotsam, finally forced me ashore.

But even that day had its compensations (it's a rare day that doesn't). By the stile, a bevy of quails, 10 or a dozen or so, ran around in sudden alarm at my appearance, then melted silently into the undergrowth. And not two minutes later, as I began the walk from the stream to my fishing at Willow Point, I caught a cock pheasant completely by surprise. He made a picture of startled, elegant and exotic perfection just there, against that wild afternoon's ragged autumnal chaos of bare, battered branches hung with untidy pennants of storm flotsam.

Only two days later, again nothing came to the fly, and absolutely nothing memorable characterised the two hours I spent there except an uncanny calm. And the calm was memorable only because it so contradicted the madcap wind and waves of two days earlier.

Today, encouraged by the rainbow scuttling for its life up the shallow stream across the beach, I changed my mind about going home early. There might be more fish waiting in the shallows to make daytime dashes. I would catch them.

If they were there, they all declined my green Hairy Dog. Half an hour of fruitless effort passed. I cast to the left, and to the right, and to the centre, time and again, and all I caught were little bits of weed and sundry rocks.

But to keep me on my toes, another carrot was dangled in front of this fishing donkey. A fish jumped, some 18 metres away. I was looking at it almost before it left the water. It jumped clean out, a 2kg fish. I can see it now, outlined against the trees on the shore. It seemed to go up and up for a long time, before falling back with a heavy, satisfying splash that echoed round the little bay.

I knew I was meant to take that leap as another good omen and carry on fishing with renewed purpose. I did nothing of the kind, however. True, I did have one last cast — no, two — in the direction of the leaper, but he had gone right away, and I went right away too, before more signs of imminent rewards could enchant me into staying any longer.

And before one or other of those shrieking paradise ducks came heading home to turn the place into purgatory again.

Winter

Farewell, Killer Bug

Waist deep at Willow Point I was, and thinking about Frank Sawyer. Well, perhaps not so much about the man as about his Killer Bug. Somewhere out there a Sawyer's Killer Bug of mine was being paraded about in the mouth of a 2kg hen rainbow trout. The fish was probably quite unconscious of the honour I had done her two mornings before; utterly oblivious of her unique status as the custodian of Lake Taupo's one and only Killer Bug. There surely couldn't be another one out there?

It hadn't all been my fault, but that didn't make the loss of my Killer Bug any less serious. I ought to have known by now that you must never hurry a good fish the last couple of metres to net or bank, particularly the kind of bank at Willow Point. It isn't really a bank at all, merely a mossy foreshore metamorphosing into water and thickly set about with bits of volcanic rock.

That morning, a peaceful lake had been so inhibiting the trout that I'd thought I might liven things up a bit by changing to a floating line carrying two small wet flies. Nothing ventured, nothing gained, they say, so I'd ventured my new 6-weight green floater, and a Killer Bug and Hedgehogger on a sinking leader, on the principle that the very slow retrieves necessary would hardly disturb the surface and alarm the fish. I wouldn't have to cast so often. Moreover, because the water is shallow at Willow Point, I believed the lightweight flies, unlike the heavy lures, would happily skim over the weed and the rocks with which the shallows are liberally littered.

True, Taupo trout in the lake feed up large on smelt (as large, in fact, as around 80 per cent of their food). But it seemed, that day, that they had decided on a temporary change of diet. Maybe, I thought, they might be desperate for Killer Bugs and Hedgehoggers? Why not? So the Killer Bug went on the point, and a Hedgehogger dropper the better part of a metre above it.

Calm continued to prevail. I was hoping against hope that a breeze from the south would spring to my rescue, to belly the line north with it and seductively dance the little flies across the bay. But no.

Too many days had lately been characterised by a moody calm, and this was another of them. The two black swans stayed entirely whole. Sometimes when you are waist deep in the lake, the swans momentarily disappear, depending on how high the waves are; but today the flat water preserved the birds in their graceful and fluting entirety.

At length a fish rose to the smooth surface 10 metres away, and I whipped the line off the water and straddled the rise with the little wet flies.

I had hardly begun to retrieve when the rod bowed thrillingly to a forceful fish. It jumped twice, and I saw that it was a portly hen rainbow of 2kg or so. But which fly had it taken? If it had chosen the Hedgehogger in that shallow water, the tail fly would probably clutch weed or rock. Was that to be the fate of my one and only Killer Bug, a gift from a visiting chalk-stream fly-fisher? On the other hand, if the fish had taken the tail fly, it might be no less difficult for Fate to bring the dropper to just as abrupt and fatal a stop. Why was I fishing two flies anyway, in such a risky place? You certainly increase your chances of catching fish by offering a choice, but just as certainly increase your chances of losing them. It's only when you hook a fish that the worry starts. You begin to heap all kinds of acrimony on yourself.

When a fish takes, you think, "Ah, well done! Land this one and we'll know which is the right fly for today." This thought works well in unobstructed water of reasonable depth; but not at Willow Point. The Hedgehogger debut, a year or so previously, sprang to mind, unbidden. That day, elated at the fast response of a hefty river rainbow to one or other — but which? — of a pair of flies, and anxious to prove straight away that Gil's Hedgehogger prototype had been chosen, I had got ready too soon to land the fish, and suffered the consequences. It would have made no difference if I had taken things calmly from start to finish. Unless that fish had snatched both flies at the same time before breaking off the encounter, his preference would be plain. So it proved, of course. It had taken the Hedgehogger dropper. And the next fish down in the pecking order in that same pool took a second Hedgehogger dropper very soon after.

That fleeting recollection of an episode which ought to have had a happier ending waved a red flag at me; but I paid no attention, anxious, again, to establish which fly had been taken. I became a little too heavy-handed, and the inevitable happened. At least, shortly before we parted company, I saw the dropper dancing on the smooth surface. So, a Sawyer's Killer Bug had made its first — and perhaps its last — conquest in Lake Taupo. I couldn't imagine anyone else ever having tried the pattern there.

The trouble is, true Killer Bugs are almost certainly extinct. They became an endangered species when Chadwick's darning wool No. 477, the all-important ingredient, went out of existence some years ago, much to the alarm of a fly-tying fraternity only just getting used to the frequently astonishing efficacy of the Sawyer bug among grayling, and then among trout.

Mind you, real wet-fly and nymphing purists wouldn't be seen dead with a Killer Bug. Cynics say Sawyer's invention is plainly a maggot. Looking at it (say on page 63 of T. Donald Overfield's book *Fifty Favourite Nymphs*), you can understand the critics' cynicism. Overfield's illustrations show a fat maggot shape tapered bluntly at both ends.

The inventor would not have been pleased with mention of maggots. Sawyer developed the pattern for grayling, knowing quite well that the result was not, strictly speaking, a nymph. But, as he says in his *Nymphs and the Trout*, grayling must be removed from trout water, even if the rules have to be stretched. He merely stretched them to imitate the freshwater shrimp, of which grayling are fond; and a very successful grayling pattern it became.

But its reputation didn't stop there. In those days of the late 1950s, when Sawyer published his *Nymphs and the Trout*, his grayling bug had no name. Five years later, in 1963, when Oliver Kite published his *Nymph Fishing in Practice*, and in it paid tribute to Sawyer's pattern, it was still only a grayling bug; but Kite made it plain that he used it successfully in big reservoirs — for trout.

Fifteen years later, in 1978, the name Killer Bug was well established — as was an even bigger reputation. Sawyer's invention dealt summarily not only with grayling but also with brown and rainbow trout in running and still waters and, believe it or not, at times with salmon.

We all know that the Englishman Frank Sawyer was an Avon riverkeeper with an exceptional understanding both of the nymphs of stream insects and of effective ways of representing them to the trout. He is most famous for his Pheasant Tail Nymph, which in 1986 was being sold and used in 60 countries. His other patterns — Grey Goose Nymph, Bow-tie Buzzer, Scandinavian Nymph and Killer Bug — enjoy lesser reputations.

Each of the five patterns was the outcome of sometimes many years of observation and experiment. Sawyer, like all the greats of the trout-fishing world, possessed remarkable eyesight. For us — his beneficiaries, so to speak — nowhere was that eyesight put to better use than along his cherished River Avon. He could see through flowing water as if no water was there. Some of us have this ability in varying degree. In him it was much more advanced than in most.

Sawyer knew all about the nymphs he watched so closely for so many

Trout-fishers all over the world value soft hackles on a wet fly. Worked under water, they move enticingly, with all the appearance of life.

Learn from the heron. He's quiet, and stealthy. He moves unhurriedly until that lightning stab. No wonder he catches a lot more fish than you or I.

New Zealand's first book of trout-fishing was written by a Christchurch barrister and published by a government anxious to attract fishermen from overseas.

S. PERCY SMITH
Surveyor General

NEW ZEALAND
SHEWING
TROUT STREAMS
1892
Scale of English Miles

th Islan

North Tarana

South Taran

TROUT IN NEW ZEALAND.
WHERE TO GO AND HOW TO CATCH THEM.
—
W. H. SPACKMAN.

Golden Bay

Tasm
Bay

HOKITIKA

Middle

Alps

CHRISTCHURCH

South

Bob Bragg's Waitaki Sedge Pupa (top), Waitaki Sedge (centre) and Gowan Nymph.

The east bank of Judge's has become an increasingly popular Tongariro pool over the past five years, particularly so for upstream nymphers.

Alex is in the process of landing yet another Taupo rainbow. As he so often does, he outfished me that day, but I more than made up for my failure the next day.

soft down plucked from its own body.

PARADISE DUCK

Maori: *Putangitangi*

Tadorna (Gmelin, 1789)
(facing page)

This species...
shooting li...
except in m...
Island, and th...
Mokau to East C...
has occurred since...

Rich reddy-browns, warm pale browns and deep blacks from a paradise duck drake, make attractive feathers for fly-tiers.

The late O. S. (Budge) Hintz, a former managing editor of the New Zealand Herald, relaxes on the bank of his beloved Waitahanui, the river running through much of his classic Trout at Taupo.

years. One of his observations told him that swimming nymphs tuck their legs into their bodies; therefore, no legs were needed on artificials. Furthermore, as he said of his shrimp pattern, having studied the natural in its underwater environment for years, no suggestion of legs was needed on that, either.

It is, then, a tiny, legless, banana-shaped artificial. Sawyer used a size 12 or 13 hook (considered large by Kite), on which he spun silver-coloured fuse wire to give weight and a pronounced hump. He left the wire dangling at the bend, then, starting at the eye, he covered the wire with an even winding of the darning wool. Two half-hitches with the wire secured the wool and the wire at the tail.

The best wool, he said, was one with a fawn background and a definite pink tinge — which, though he did not mention a make or shade in *Nymphs and the Trout*, must have been Chadwick's No. 477, the wool specified in subsequent fly-tying manuals.

Now, if Sawyer's Killer Bug isn't the simplest tie (but one) of any trout fly (the exception being Kite's Bare Hook Nymph), I'll eat my fishing hat. His three nymph patterns were equally simple. Sawyer was a man who cut the number and complexity of nymph patterns virtually to the bone, and moreover advocated using readily obtainable, inexpensive materials.

More importantly for anglers and angling historians, it was Sawyer who introduced to fly-tying the concept of using fine copper wire or fuse wire in place of tying silk when nymphs needed weighting to get them down to the trout.

Waist deep at Willow Point, two days after my Killer Bug had gone swimabout, I reflected on the chances of catching the same fish and recovering the fly. The odds were mind-boggling, but that's what Lotto winners say, too. The closest I, personally, had come to such a miracle was on a fishing day in Turangi. Going up the Boulevard, I hooked a fish and held it too hard. The tippet parted at the fly. Ten minutes later I hooked another fish — in the back. When I landed it I was able to recover two nymphs, one from the back and one from the mouth. Both were mine.

Would Fate step in and restore my Killer Bug to me? The day was already enchanted. Warm winter sunshine masquerading as spring sunshine, tuis and bellbirds and grey warblers calling behind me, and a peace so much more perfect for an absence of paradise duck and spur-winged plover racket, almost persuaded me that Fate might be looking kindly on the possibility of restoration. Mind you, the soft southerly breeze exasperatingly kept on coming and going. I changed lines twice to match the wind.

I fished a size 8 Red Setter fast, and slow. In the calm of a lengthy lull I hooked a doughty fish. It let go. And then, in 10 minutes of ripple, right at the end of a slow retrieve, I was suddenly playing another fish, a small, fat, rainbow hen, only half the size of the bearer of my Killer Bug. I drew her onto the mossy shore and, dentist-like, peered into her mouth. Only the Red Setter sat there.

I would have to scour the Taupo wool shops for a light, greyish-brown darning wool with a pink tinge . . .

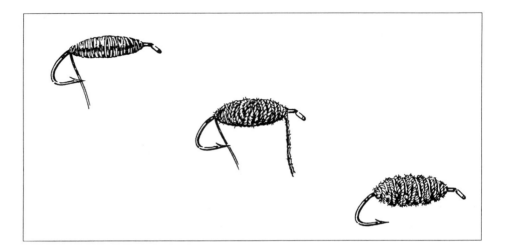

The slower he goes, the more he sees

Although they speak of England, some words in one of Robert Gibbings' lovely books, *Sweet Thames Run Softly*, encapsulate universal truths for those of us who want to see behind the veil that so often masks the face of Nature. At the same time, they at once recall to me a fisherman of New Zealand.

Firstly, here is Robert Gibbings' gentle advice: "Learn to walk slowly, so that we have time to see."

Only a month ago, Jim Ackerley of Ashburton wrote to ask a small favour. Could I tell him the name of the scholarly American and the title of the fishing book he had written which Jim and I had discussed some years previously during his search for a modern text of Dame Juliana's classic?

His letter told me, among other things, that he was getting old. He wasn't able to move as fast these days. But then he said: "The slower I go, the more I see."

What a happy thought! And what a lot those simple words tell of Jim Ackerley's philosophy, and of his regard for the natural world about him.

At home, Margaret and I often — but not often enough — take the walk along Wakeman Road, down the steps into Acacia Bay, and then north towards Taupo, until Besley Place takes us back into Wakeman Road again. Sometimes I walk the circuit alone, and when I do it is always taken at speed, to help me keep in shape for the sometimes strenuous walks of the Taupo Weekday Walkers.

Robert Gibbings would not be impressed by these shows of physical exertion, either mine or the weekday walkers', if our aim is to come close to Nature. But then, that isn't our aim, and in some ways more's the pity. We are walking for health and pleasure. Because the Taupo Weekday Walkers sometimes number 60 and more, we have no time to stand and stare. Anyway, we chatter away like starlings while the going's good, but Nature knows very well we are no kind of birds at all at all, and prudently distances herself from our advance.

Gibbings' four lines draw attention to the need for silence if we are to see Nature, so he might not have cared to walk with us. He says: "We must learn to tread quietly, so that we do not cause alarm . . ." He ends that thought with the words: "above all, we must *think* peace".

Five days at Turangi

Faint breezes blew as I drove to Turangi on the last day of July for five days of fishing and photography. By midday I was sheathed in chest waders and on my way to Cunningham's Corner.

That year, as if to warn of what was to come, much more water was streaming down the bypass (originally the main course of the river) under the long curving cliff from the Stag Pool down. In fact, crossing over the bypass at Cunningham's looked distinctly risky, and I didn't attempt it. It wouldn't be long before the bypass indeed became the main course of the river once again, denying anglers access to some fine water on a miniature Tongariro.

The Sallow Pool had gone, but above it was now a long, deep pool which was eminently fishable from either bank. A downstreamer on my side had just landed one mediocre fish, having lost three others. Above him, two nymphers were fishing opposite Cunningham's.

I pottered around for a while and later fished the pool where the downstreamer had hooked his four. Apart from a brief acquaintance with a fish, I hooked nothing except one snag — three times. It was interesting that the tapered and foreshortened German leader broke each time at the join with the heavier French nylon. I had always regarded that German stuff as treacherously brittle, and once again I was proved right. Why continue to use it then?

That last day of July was wintry, and yet it spoke undeniably of spring here and there. I had heard a chaffinch singing his spring song in the motel grounds; hesitantly mind, but no more hesitantly than one in the garden at home which I had first heard, would you believe, in the middle of the month.

Unhappily for me, many anglers were about. From the Hydro up I counted eight on my side. The river was rather high, and showing a fair amount of colour, but it was unquestionably fishable. Just before dark I explored downstream from the motel. The water on the other side of Judge's looked very good indeed. I would try it first thing in the morning.

I did, nymphing it up twice between 8.30 and 9.30 and landing two fish, first a hefty jack of 1.5kg, and then a fresh-run hen of about the same weight.

I couldn't enthuse over the weather. It was dour and wet. It had rained all night, and it continued to do so the whole time I was fishing.

Colour tinged the water later in the day, but at no stage did it become unfishable. After lunch I fished the same pool again, this time with a lure worked downstream, and briefly encountered two fish. In the normal course of events I think I would have landed one of the two, but the hook of the Red Setter unaccountably straightened out. Unaccountably? Well, no doubt a tempering failure was the cause of that lost fish.

Clearly, fish lay in that pool, but their indifference surprised me. Why weren't they more forthcoming? Was I not fishing the lure properly? One of the reasons I had chosen to fish the lure after lunch rather than persevere with the nymph was the memory of the occasion in the same area when a downstreamer's lure had worked so much better than my nymph, possibly because, as Bill and I later reasoned, fish fresh from the lake would be far more ready to take a small-fish imitation than an artificial insect larva.

My two sessions in the pool each gave me a full hour of fishing undisturbed by others. Only one angler turned up later in the morning, and one in the afternoon. Both were downstreamers, and luckily they were both older men, like myself. Each of them knew his river etiquette, and quietly observed it. If only everyone did the same.

The after-lunch occasion with the lure was interesting, but after a while I changed back to the floater, and within half an hour had hooked two fish. The first, possibly a jack, came unstuck as I was trying to land it. The second was a very modestly proportioned hen weighing at most a kilo, and yet she hurtled away downstream as though twice as big, and fought and fought.

The nymphs that day were Keith Gallaugher's Hare and Coppers. Keith used to say they never did any good for him, but they certainly did well enough for me.

By the greatest good luck, no-one happened to be fishing the Major Jones towards the end of the morning, and I nymphed it up, feeling, never-the-less, an interloper in that domain of the traditional downstreamer. Quite rightly, perhaps, the fish were only prepared to consider lures, for nothing came to the Hare and Copper.

When the rain stopped after lunch, fair-weather fishermen metamorphosed in droves — well, half a dozen at least — but the weather made no difference to the local thrushes. That day, rain or shine, they sang their hearts out. Grey warblers sang too, and once a chaffinch, and at some time as I slowly worked my way down the Major Jones behind a Red Setter, thinking of Geoff Sanderson, I turned round at an odd noise behind me and found two herons fighting on the bank.

Last year's great flood, which changed so many features of the river, is still much in evidence. Coupled with the flotsam and jetsam of winter, flood-wrack imposes a desolate appearance on the river and its banks. You begin to understand the difference between chalk streams and flood-prone rivers only after the kind of rearrangement Nature in New Zealand makes during a time of sustained heavy rain.

All right, it was winter, but it was something of a shock to wake up to a really cold morning the next day. Milk was frozen solid in the fridge (was the weather to blame, though, or the fridge?) and snow lay halfway down Mt Pihanga. I had never seen snow that far down the mountain before.

Snow showers fell during the day; showers of anglers, too. At eight o'clock, after breakfast, I was two anglers too late to secure sole posses-

131

sion of the true right bank of Judge's. They were downstreaming the pool, and I left them to it, deciding to follow my original plan for the day, which was mainly to photograph and catch fishing pictures rather than fish.

I went as far as the Blue Pool, and because so many anglers were about, I caught fishing pictures all the way, while the southerly whistled downriver and snow showers drew grey-white curtains over the hills. Towards evening, the southerly relented, but anglers persisted in the places I wanted to fish. In fact, there was only one place I was able to squeeze into — behind a downstreamer in Judge's, where I nymphed up towards the Island.

Word was that fish were being caught in the Hydro in some quantity. I didn't check out the Hydro, but I did see fish landed here and there in the neighbourhood. None was returned, so the anglers were almost certainly visitors. Two fish were dealt with quite barbarically. They weren't killed straightaway. I was concerned. Surely by now the word had spread that if you're going to keep a fish you kill it mercifully quickly, instead of letting it gasp its life out on the bank?

Because it was Saturday, fishing pressure was considerable, despite the weather. Harry's Rock sported six anglers, the Cliff four and the Fan two. Three anglers were trying conclusions in the tail of the Blue, and two at the head. I might have fished Big Bend, but just before I left to go back to the car and tackle up, I caught the distant shine of rod varnish from that direction: someone was already fishing there.

I know now what I ought to have done the following day, Sunday (hindsight is always so clear). I ought to have done what I had actually planned to do — take photographs rather than compete with the mob. I wish I wasn't so often wise after the event . . .

The day had opened with such a flat and uninteresting light, with the sky so blurred with low cloud, that I gave away the idea of photography and drove to the Red Hut Bridge, where a score of cars bore testimony to the fact that it was Sunday and that rumour had it the river held plenty of running fish.

One angler returned to his car with a limit of good-looking fish — caught, he said, in the Red Hut Pool itself. He could have had a couple of limits, but had lost a lot. Three men were nymphing at the tail of the pool, on the highway side of the river, when I clumped down the steps to the bridge.

I had planned to walk downstream on the highway side of the river, without crossing the bridge, and find a way down to that interesting big pocket of water on the way to the Shag Pool, but fresh thoughts waylaid me, and I finished up crossing the bridge after all and heading towards

Waddell's. After Waddell's, I thought, I would find my way to Boulder Reach and fish that up — a favourite stretch of mine.

Waddell's had changed; and I was pipped at the post. A young angler materialised ahead of me, and someone was following up behind me. I fished the pool hurriedly. It was bigger now, and seemingly not so far above the bridge as it once had been; but there was an eddy problem still.

So to the Poutu Pool, where no fewer than four were fishing. Two of them were nymphing, and one had landed five fish between 1.8kg and 2.2kg each.

I didn't think it was all that cold, and I suppose with neoprene chest waders, two jerseys, a jacket, a fishing vest and a parka, I wasn't mistaken; but it suddenly began to snow, quietly and softly, at the Poutu. I left the four fishermen to it.

Boulder Reach was Glo-bug Alley today. Fish lay for the most part in the fast shallows at the tail of the reach, and in the jobbly water down the true left bank. But, once he had put on a Glo-bug, the nympher halfway up the other bank began to hook fish. While I was there he lost a good one and landed a long, slim hen. I helped him beach a jack of 2kg or so when I came back from the Fan, where I hadn't got a touch. Chris had had the Fan to himself for some hours, and had landed two fish and lost two. Two nymphers opposite me, towards the tail of Boulder Reach, both using Glo-bugs, landed possibly 10 fish. They had started on my side, and been immediately successful, but their success had drawn so many other anglers to them that they had abandoned the place and sought the comparative peace of the true left bank.

The snow didn't fall for very long that day, but it helped make the occasion of the Glo-bugs a memorable one, if not for me, then certainly for those who used them. Although I had had the Fan to myself, Boulder Reach was being fished by seven nymphers when I finally came away, fishless.

The motel understandably likes guests to book out punctually, so I had just a couple of hours of fishing on the last morning of my Turangi stay, and I chose to spend it nymphing the "other side" of Judge's. I don't think anyone had fished the pool before me that morning.

I could have done with some big and hefty nymphs, but at that stage of the stay in Turangi, I only had a few size 12s left. I put two on, one looped to the hook of the other, and began working upstream.

A small fish came first. A larger fish fastened on inside 15 minutes, and I had almost played it out when the hook came away. Ten minutes later a third fish took, and bolted for its life across the fast broken water at the head of the pool. It jumped high — and threw the hook. I chuckled, and it was time to go.

Swallows had woven endless flight patterns across the river everywhere; and in the mornings the thrushes had sung, and sung, and sung.

Biter bit

Two hours after the event, I am now sure the blood was mine. It wasn't the trout's. It was on the outside of his mouth, so it must have been mine, although at the time of releasing him and seeing the blood I felt a sudden pang: he would surely die.

But three of his needle-sharp teeth had punctured my left thumb, and blood flowed freely as I tweaked the Red Setter from the fly's small grip on a bloodless pinch of skin on the roof of the trout's mouth.

I wrapped a handkerchief round the thumb, feeling bewildered but pleasantly surprised at the way things were going. Whakaipo was wiping the slate clean. Four recent outings had brought me no fish at all, not even the faintest touch of a fish. As ever, though, the bay for me was alive with interest, even though on two of those occasions I could have done without the interest gratuitously offered by screaming paradise ducks.

Two hours after the trout bit me, I am thinking of the day as a fish-sandwich day. A thick slice of empty endeavour began it. Then a sudden fish-filling sumptuously arrived. After that, too soon, another slice of empty endeavour followed. I would like to have made it a club sandwich, but two slices and one layer of filling were all I was allowed.

Not too many compensations for the single filling lay around. But the lake was beautifully full, and the Mapara Stream went rollicking, brown-stained, into it. We'd had heavy rain showers in the morning, followed by a clear blue sky. Then those sometimes great wet masses, sometimes dirty grey walls, and sometimes straggly patches, of cloud, loomed over from the west. A small continuous chop rode steadily up the eastern shore of the bay.

When I came creeping down the track from the stile, grimacing already at the paradise duck that was bound to be there, waiting to shriek her abhorrence of creeping fishermen, a heron saw me first. It carried on fishing. I moved out from the camouflaging shrubs and a shag leapt for

134

its life from the side of the brown stream. Was it there waiting for a precocious small jack or two to scuttle up from the lake?

Thank Heaven, no paradise ducks were patrolling. No black swans, either. For months, a family of five swans has made the bay its domain. Little did the five of them know that at times when they sailed curiously past this waist-deep fisherman, he could have stroke-hauled any one of them from the water if his hook had held.

The rushing stream persuaded me to fish the broad swathe of stained water it was hurrying into the lake. An hour of casting and retrieving passed pleasantly enough, but it would have been nice to have topped it off with a fish. Often, at this midwinter time of year, when the stream comes tumbling boisterously for a change into the lake, fish congregate, ready at the coming of darkness to run the gauntlet of the open beach and gain the safety of the green fastnesses so close, on their way up to spawn.

But not today. No fish intercepted the Red Setter. No fish showed. A barren, brown stream was rushing into a barren, brown lake. Then a kingfisher went by, so at least there were tiny fish to catch. Someone must

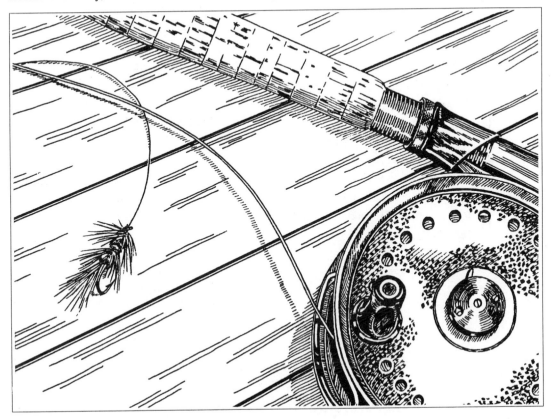

have caught all the bigger ones.

It was time to make a move to Willow Point. I walked and waded round, looking at the recently coloured brown-topped stones in the water, squishing on land the slippery new layers of soft, dark-green bobbles that the big westerlies wash up out of the lake.

Mindful of the last time but four at Willow Point, when I started roll-casting almost before emerging from under the bare branches of the willow, and hooked a fish straightaway, I edged out ankle deep and put out a roll-cast of 6 or 7 metres.

You have to wade out 10 metres or so to find waist-deep water, but after what happened today I may not bother in future, particularly in times of high water. Maybe fish were there today because the lake had come up quickly, weed had rotted away, and small aquatic fauna had come foraging into the new shallows, drawing trout after them. Maybe the fish that were there hadn't looked at the fishing calendar; the day was one of 11 in June branded "Bad". Maybe the fish were always there but needed to be approached on only faintly choppy days with the utmost caution.

I remembered something about the stream-mouth. A one-time manager of the local radio station, a keen and knowledgeable night-time fly-fisher, finding no other cars parked under the pines at Whakaipo, would creep down the track from the stile and make his first casts as far back from the undisturbed water as possible. This is difficult at the stream-mouth because the trees crowd you from behind, especially if the lake is high. One night, just in front of him, he hooked a 3.6kg brown trout on his first cast, and a 3.6kg brown trout on his second cast. He landed both, and he hadn't got his feet wet.

Thinking about such cautionary tales, I lifted the rod to make a somewhat longer roll-cast. The fly snagged. Damn that rock, I thought. And then the rock shook its head, and jumped, and five minutes later I slid a jack rainbow of 1.6kg up the slippery green bobbles. Hurrah for cautionary tales!

That jack wasn't the fish that bit me. That was the next one. I had stealthily gone in again after shepherding the freed rainbow back to deeper water, and was standing calf deep with almost 10 metres of line out. The sky looked as though it would drench Whakaipo Bay any minute; indeed, heavy drops began to fall. Next moment, a fish clamped on the Red Setter, a dour one, without acrobatics or imagination. The light was so bad now that when the fish rolled over on its way in to the beach I thought it was an old slab; but it was a fine jack brown trout of close to 2.2kg, all dusky gold, quite unlike the only other brown I'd caught just there, another 2.2kg fish, all silver, with a few dark spots.

Calf deep again, a few minutes later, with a handkerchief round my bleeding thumb, I heard a slurping noise to my left. No deeper than I was, the fish was sucking at the surface, so I quickly gave it something else to suck at. It grabbed the fly, the line went taut, but the rod had hardly bent before the fly came away again.

Perhaps I ought to have gone ashore, rested the place for 20 minutes or so, and then, ankle deep, roll-cast my way back to the stream-mouth. Yes, that's what I ought to have done. Instead, I waded deeper and cast 20 metres of line here, there and everywhere into what my sunglasses transformed from silver waves into bronze. I did that for an hour or so, and was utterly unrewarded. That was the second fish-sandwich slice of empty endeavour.

To think that the delicious filling in between had taken only 25 minutes!

Two hours later, the punctures under my band-aided thumb remind me of the rabbit I saw splattered bloodily on the road to Whakaipo on the way out. A harrier hawk rose unwillingly from the gory mess: after all, it wasn't going to try conclusions with a car on the same side of the road.

It was a different matter coming back. The hawk was busy disposing of the corpse again. I slowed right down. It stuck to its feast, wings threateningly hunched forward, eyes malevolently on me, daring me to stop and wrest the rabbit from it. I gave it best and drove off before it could fly into the open window and puncture other bits of my anatomy.

Two from The Point

You don't have to get your feet wet to catch trout at The Point, but you do need a long-handled landing net to land them.

The Point is the name of the exclusive Taupo residential estate being developed just west of Whakamoenga Point, on the northern shore of Mine Bay, by the Gower family. It lies in 23.5 hectares of small trees and shrubs rising up from the lake and facing south to the cliffs of Karangahape and the distant southern townships of Turangi and Tokaanu. Standing up tall well beyond the nearer horizon down there lie the three great peaks of Tongariro National Park.

Naturally, the view down the lake from the higher points of this residential amphitheatre is magnificent — but not much more so than the fisherman's view, from just above water level, from the recreation reserve below.

Somewhere among the minor memorabilia a man tucks away over the years, I still have a key to the gate that used to deny access to most visitors to Whakamoenga Point. Many Taupo anglers who also had keys would by now have thrown them away, for the old padlocked gate that led to the little fishing paradise of Whakamoenga, or The Rocks, as some call it, has been replaced by grand ornamental gates which can only be opened with an electronic key.

The little fishing paradise is still there, however, and open to all. Gone, certainly, is the sense of ownership with which you let yourself into the property, locked the gate behind you, and drove down the narrow lane past some of Robin Jansen's Acacia Bay Apiaries hives, tackled up close to a diesel generator shed, and plunged into the bushes and down the path to paradise.

The Gowers' house on the property was vandalised so many times by local louts, who would break down the gate and smash a way into the house, or at best leave piles of broken beer bottles and smoking campfires as tokens of their esteem for private property and the environment, that you would suppose a degree of reluctance on the part of the owners would inhibit any further desire to preserve the privilege they had extended to fishermen for so many years.

Not a bit of it. They like fishermen. Fishermen were not to blame for the vandalism, so why penalise them? The Gowers gritted their teeth and repaired the damage and cleaned up yet again; and still allowed more keys to be cut for fishermen.

You don't need even an electronic key now, and fishermen aren't the only people who are welcome to enjoy the walk out to favourite fishing and picnicking places and the views down the lake.

For the Gowers, bless them, donated land along the edge of the lake to make a recreation reserve for the general public; and the Department of Conservation formed and signposted a track from the new roadside car park on the Taupo side of The Point gates to join up with an old track on the Gower property leading out to the point itself.

As a serious trout-fisher alone or in company, or a trout-fisher on a family picnic or walk, you will find that Whakamoenga Point makes an interesting change from rushing rivers or crowded Taupo beaches. Park

138

your car, 15 minutes after leaving town, at the new car park way beyond Acacia Bay and shortly before you get to The Point gates, and take the signposted mini bush walk to Whakamoenga Point. Ten minutes on the way, two small beaches invite a stay, but most people continue for another 10 minutes or so to Mine Bay and the views south and east, and the prospect of fish in the deep water surrounding the point itself.

Yes, it is like fishing off a wharf, but it is fishing which is not particularly demanding — ideal, for instance, for youngsters serving a spin-fishing apprenticeship. It is often well rewarded, too. Sometimes the wind will decide which side of the point will be more productive, particularly when smelt are in evidence. If smelt are about, you will best fish smelt flies and retrieve them fast on a floating or slow-sinking line.

Usually, though, and especially in the depth of winter or the heat and glare of summer days, combing the bottom with a bushy lure fished as a bully brings the most frequent responses. You need a fast-sinking line, and so often only a size 8, or even a size 10, Red Setter, and a watch to time the most productive depth at which to fish, for the undulating platform of rock you are fishing off drops practically vertically to a depth of 11 metres in most places around the point.

In earlier days, when my old medium-sinking line was still in its prime, I used to allow two minutes for the line to sink before beginning a retrieve. The fast-sinker I am using now drops like a stone, so one day recently I was allowing just over a minute for the lure to reach what I hoped might be a level at which trout were looking for food.

The place, in theory, seemed entirely appropriate. A strong easterly driving waves at the eastern face of Whakamoenga's bulwarks spent itself on that side; and the waves, once around the corner into the more sheltered bay, diminished in size and urgency. Would there not be fish patrolling the quieter waters, on the lookout for smelt and bullies seeking less boisterous quarters?

There were. My pleasure in that rocky promontory and its deep waters was enhanced by the catching of two rainbows within an hour of arrival — one of 1.3kg, and a bigger one of 1.6kg. The smaller of the two, a jack, was in good condition. He ran hard three times, once taking me well into the backing. He captured the little Red Setter well down in the water. The other fish, a hen, lacked the condition of the jack. She was full of eggs, but eggs only about a fifth of the size one would expect for the time of year. Oddly, she took the lure high in the water, towards the end of a retrieve.

Those two rainbows made two thirds of a present-day limit. I kept them

139

both, not too concerned that, for a change, I was killing what I caught. Lake fish have always seemed fair game, but I rarely keep river fish. Strange, that.

Real cool at The Hotspot

Even The Hotspot let me down. Just on the off chance that it might redeem two hours of inactivity on the part of the trout, I fished it for 10 minutes on my way back to the car. As I fished, the sun sank below the western hills, and the water in the bay quietened and quietened until the surface reflected only the darkness of the dusky hillsides, darkness broken only by the rare silver gleam of a dying ripple.

Fleetingly, after a mug of sweet tea and some chocolate, and a return to the water at the northern end of Gillett's Bay, I had tensed as a fish took hold. But it let go. I speeded up the retrieve, but it did not come again.

I know several fishermen who would have preferred to wipe the slate clean of today's fishing had it been theirs. I pity them for their single-mindedness. Their belief that the sole purpose of going fishing is to catch fish makes them castaways on an island barren of angling enjoyments. Their only enjoyment, it seems, is the landing of fish. The more they land, the greater their enjoyment, but only if they can prove to their peers, and perhaps to their children too, that indeed they are equal to any angling challenge. That kind of demonstration smacks of the macho syndrome, which on the one hand breeds champion round-the-world sailors, champion rugby teams, first-class racing drivers, horsemen, rowers and so on, but on the other hand breeds contempt for people who don't subscribe to the win-at-all-costs philosophy. It's the syndrome that believes fishing is a game to be won rather than a pastime to be enjoyed.

For a change, there were certainly fish about today. I saw four or five broach. One slurped at the surface after a small fish, within casting distance. Harry had preceded me to the bay and was fishing off Willow Point, hoping, no doubt, to connect with the fish that had jumped out when he arrived and fallen back again with the impact of a bag of cement.

I went on to Gillett's Bay. A slight, cool breeze from the south drove a steady ripple north. Virtually all the time I fished I faced the sun. I had brought the wrong hat for the water dazzle, and this evening my eyes are sore in consequence, but I have no regrets. The afternoon was a wonderful experience for anyone who could see beyond a blinkered compulsion to take fish home.

To begin with, as always at Whakaipo on any sunny winter afternoon without a strong wind, the side of the bay facing the sun sat like a child sitting cosily in front of the fire. That side — the side I wade and fish so enjoyably — must turn into spring much sooner than the other side, which is steep and shadowed, and drops sharply into deep water; a shore I believe to be practically inaccessible except by boat.

My side rang with the songs of birds today — whiteheads, tuis, bell-birds. Already, tuis were soaring and plummeting over the lake-side trees. From time to time four of them rose and dived, one or other of them crying in that shrill, plaintive way that tuis have when upset about something. So spring is on the way, and the starling's egg I found on the ground in town two days ago is after all not so surprising; and in four or five places over recent days, I have watched cock blackbirds shaping up to one another in territorial squabbles.

As if to confound a recent belief of mine that kingfishers must have deserted the bay altogether, at least two made their appearance now and again. They perched in willows not too far back now from the lake edge: since the other day the water has risen a good 12cm. Already the unsightly piles of weed, like heaps of green porridge, have subsided, improving the look of the northeast corner of the bay considerably.

Drinking tea at the nearer end of Gillett's Bay, I recalled a time not so long ago when the dead willow trunk I was sitting on formed a living part of a very substantial tree just there. Surely the lake lapped almost to the bole of the tree in those days? I remembered how the ground there ran smoothly into the water, all mossy-green, ridged with the long willow roots that radiated thirstily in all directions. Those same roots were still there, but the ground had shrunk away, revealing small rocks, and the roots were dead and broken.

I didn't realise until recently how short-lived the Whakaipo Bay willows are — well, at least the ones along the shore I fish. Quite five or six big and seemingly healthy trees have died in the past 15 years. They will never die out of course, because branches break off in the gales that batter the northern shores and take root alongside the parent trees.

Ominously again, today, I saw no small fish at all. Not a single smelt or bully. Ominously, too, far fewer koura carapaces litter the shoreline these days. But if the presence of shags proves the presence of small fish and koura, then food for shags must be there in abundance, for at least 20 of them scurried away from the Gillett's Bay rocks when I approached.

The one fish that I might have caught — the one that groped and splashed at the surface, presumably in chase of a small fish — most probably saw the Hairy Dog I flung in its path. But that cast happened to become the second in possibly 150 I had already made which presented a lure with its tail wrapped round the bend of the hook. I might have done a great deal better without that particular Hairy Dog anyway, for it stubbornly refused to sink properly. I did try a small Taupo Tiger too, but found myself angrily giving it a quick haircut very soon after tying it on, for it began to wrap almost immediately.

By the time I reached The Hotspot the sun was dropping down behind the hills. The breeze died away. The Hairy Dog wouldn't sink, and swam on the surface back to me as I retrieved. I was so disgusted with it that I actually finished off the afternoon with only one last cast. Usually, of course, two or three are obligatory, sometimes more; but that Hairy Dog was made to suffer for its sins.

Snug, but unrewarded

At times it poured today. Mostly, though, low cloud merely settled damply all around, like a sort of upstairs fog. Once or twice, when a faint breeze adzed the water, the fog lifted, but then the breeze died and the water lay quite flat.

Someone had confined the stream within two rows of small rocks so that it ran narrowly out of the little overgrown valley and rushed the last few metres across the beach and into the lake. Two black swans, out on the calm surface, called a greeting. The lake was disagreeably low. Piles of pulverised green weed lay round the northeastern corner, smelling offensively. Was the smell stronger today? If so, was it because some of it was water-net weed? The northeastern corner of the bay would seem to offer virtually ideal conditions for this newly arrived and most undesirable plant.

At such times as this one thinks of weather the very opposite of that of today. Instead of clammy grey cloud and an overall colourless prospect, and mounds of stinking green weed along the shore, I wanted to see a sunlit landscape halfway through spring, with the willow leaves moving in a steady small breeze, and the waves riding past from the southwest, and the lake at a level far higher than today's.

I fished from 2.30pm or so until around 5.00pm, snug in my Barbour

jacket with the hood up. For a change I'd put thigh boots on, and took jolly good care I didn't wade very deep and get the jacket wet.

A fish nipped at the Taupo Tiger at 4.00pm. I speeded up the retrieve straightaway, and the fish came a second time, but not with enough determination to allow me to make lasting contact.

Strangely, shortly after I arrived, just as I was wondering whether, for a change at Whakaipo, I would see evidence of fish, something broached a mere 7 metres away. I cast the Taupo Tiger to it, but no pull came. And that was Whakaipo on this cold and clammy midwinter afternoon.

Snow on a Red Setter day

Taupo is agog. For the first time in more than 30 years, snow has turned Mt Tauhara's green farmland white, and blanketed the hills at the back of Acacia Bay and right round from there to Wairakei. Cars full of celebrating families are out and about to catch the phenomenon before it melts from their grasp.

They say the snow fell very late last night and very early this morning. Certainly nothing white lay on the hills as I drove back from Whakaipo Bay late yesterday afternoon. True, it was cold. I was cold too, and that was not really surprising. I had been standing in the bay up to my chest for two hours, casting a little Red Setter time and time again across what small ripples undulated north past me, and then retrieving the fly enticingly in small darts and dashes.

Deep wading was obligatory. Every other year or so I write around this time that I have never seen the lake so high. So it was again yesterday, and blessedly so; and surely it had never been as high before?

All the stinking piles of weed at the water's edge, and all the grubby metres of rock-studded foreshore between the water and the trees, had given way to cleansing, clear, cold water. The higher the water rises, however, the closer the wading fisherman is forced back towards the trees behind him. Those trees reach out greedy hands for the back-cast fly. Luckily, yesterday, because I manoeuvred carefully about to fish in front of the one or two small inlets along the shore, the trees caught me out only once.

Encouragingly, a trout came solidly to the little Red Setter within 10 minutes of starting. It was a hard-fighting but small fish of a kilo or so. Then the breeze diminished. The water in the bay smoothed out, and the branches of the willows, which had been cheerfully waving modest new green bannerets at the awakening year, relapsed into immovability. Lambs cried reedily from the paddocks, and thrushes practised for spring. I thought of the welcome tinkling song of the dunnock I had heard in the garden that morning.

But you have to take the rough of the awakening year with the smooth. One or two sleepy blowflies, harbingers of the hordes to come, proved the point.

A lazy, lengthening shower came up soon on another breeze, and all of a sudden a second fish was bucking out there, while the two resident black swans looked on amazed.

With the lake so high, landing fish at Whakaipo becomes a problem. The tippet would break at 3kg. My fish would have weighed no more than 1.5kg, but I had my doubts whether I should land it. Fortunately, the wall of trees and scrub is not a solid one. If it were, a landing net would have been essential. I ought to have had one with me in any case.

I guided the uplifted rod between the grasping branches of two trees,

and slid the fish up a little beach of detritus and drowned grass.

It was a silvery rainbow trout, whose shapely bulk almost determined me to savour it smoked on the table one day soon. But there were three good rainbows in the freezer already, from the time I had outfished Alex, for once, at Whakaipo; so I disengaged the Red Setter and sent the fish back. I carry that trout's shape and bulk in my mind's eye now, but whether the third trout I took merely sprang from the same mould, or was indeed fish number two eager for another helping of Red Setter, I shall never know.

It would have been nice to know, too, whether that particular Red Setter from the fly box was the one I had flavoured with Vegemite two weeks ago — purely in the interests of MAF science and scientists, of course. They had recently proved that Marmite is surprisingly attractive as a bait for freshwater fish and invertebrates. True. But maybe there is a subtle difference between Vegemite and Marmite (although the scientists didn't really think so), for my Vegemite-impregnated Red Setter failed miserably.

By coincidence, today, all three fish took the fly into the right-hand corner of the mouth. Again, my mind's eye sees each one on its left side being drawn up on the drowned grass under the trees, and the orange body of the little Red Setter glowing hotly in the uppermost corner of its mouth.

Statistics are important

A girl from DoC popped breathlessly into view a couple of metres away.

One moment I was alone, cursing the fly-fisher out of earshot far below who had waded out of the Tongariro just as I was about to photograph him; the next a girl sprang up like a Jill-in-the-box from the steep climb to the high top of the west-bank cliff between the Boulder Pool and the Fan Pool. She carried a fish-measuring board, a walkie-talkie and a clipboard.

Today was one of the randomly selected days of the Department of Conservation's survey of Tongariro River anglers. Statistics collected by DoC staff this day would figure in a thoroughly comprehensive scientific Lake Taupo trout population survey. I was angler number 17 on the girl's clipboard. Only three of us had caught fish, very early that morning. I was not one of them. I had fished on and off, and photographed on and off, for

four hours. I could claim a catch of a fine photograph or two, but no fish.

The day was magnificent in its sharp, sunny, early-spring splendour. From the top of the cliff the girl from DoC and I paid brief homage to the dazzling white mountains rising up beyond Pihanga's southern slopes, and then she was gathering her survey gear together and plunging off down the track to the Boulder Pool and more statistics.

Not too many trout-fishers were about really, but they numbered enough to sour this angler's day. I had hoped to fish up Boulder Reach, and I came to it by way of Waddell's, because Waddell's was empty of anglers.

No fish responded to my casting virtuosity or my caddis imitation there, so I went on up to the Poutu Pool, where three anglers had fished without reward for some hours.

Changes in banks and flows and pools greeted me wherever I went, for of course a considerable flood had come down the Tongariro only a few weeks before. Fishermen had hardly adjusted to the changes wrought by the previous 3-metre flood when the new one swept down to the lake almost as high.

When I came to the tail end of Boulder Reach and looked up its length, the long line of curving bank appeared to be tenanted by only one angler, a distant nympher apparently anchored to the rock below the really big rock at the top of the reach. I had already made my way into position to fish a nymph up towards the other man when a second angler appeared and calmly got into the water 50 metres upstream. Damn and damn and damn. These days though, and very sadly, 50 metres is a long way between anglers on the Tongariro.

From the top of the cliff I could see the little man with the tremendously long cast who had been fishing the Fan Pool all morning. He had earlier lost one fish and foul-hooked another and returned it. Well below him I could just make out the first of the five immovable nymphers I knew were fishing the ever-popular Breakaway Pool.

The Fan seemed to be a pool much improved by the floods. I hoped that one day soon I would find no-one fishing it. Perhaps it would be another of DoC's randomly selected days of survey. Perhaps, if I were able to select randomly two or three fish from the pool, they would boost the figures. If nothing else, they would certainly boost this angler's ego.

Rain, rain, go away . . .

Fine rain sweeps in from the northeast on the wings of a fitful breeze driving an endless succession of waves across the bay.

We have had far too much of it, this persistent rain, for the better part of five weeks. Not every day, but most days, we have experienced fine rain, heavy rain, scattered showers or haar-like drizzle, all perversely set on dirtying the rivers and raising the lake.

Naturally, it has been most welcome, but enough is enough. The lake is comfortably full again (it rose exactly a metre in four weeks), the mountains to the south are so deep under snow that skiers have been unable to reach the slopes, and the new green mantles of the awakening year are already overinsured against dehydration.

Surprisingly, the seasonal scattering of pollen from Taupo's pine trees has not been inhibited by the damp weather. You would think it would not drift far from the trees themselves. True, our nearest pines stand barely 400 metres away on top of the rise to the west, but it's more than ever a surprise this year to find, day by day, new lines of bright greenish-yellow pollen washed down the cobblestones ready for the next heavy rain to flush them away into the stormwater drain.

It's a time, too, for camellia blooms to decay and fall, for I am told they don't like prolonged and heavy rain. Our camellias are covered in pinky-red blooms, most of which look decidedly the worse for their ordeal by rain. Huge, decaying blooms litter the grass under the shrubs, having succumbed even earlier to the ageing process.

Some of our kowhai flowers have also succumbed, but not to the ageing process. Five tuis sipping in the tree yesterday morning early did no perceivable harm. It was the other nectar-sipper that, perhaps inadvertently, pulled flowers off the tree. At first, I wondered about the square-ended brown tail poking up from behind a screen of flowers, leaves and seed-pods. It seemed an odd colour, and an odd size, for a tui. It stayed in position, vertically, for half a minute, and then one of the tuis plunged at it. Up came a complete surprise — a kaka!

The tuis did not like him there at all. Every now and again one of the five would lunge at the bigger bird, but he showed no signs of dismay or anger. He just kept flopping about among the blossoms, reaching forward with his upper mandible to anchor a particular flower so that his lower mandible, used as a scoop, could milk the bloom of its nectar.

149

I wonder whether he was the same kaka I saw in the trees on the bank some weeks ago. Acacia Bay does not seem a specially appropriate environment for a kaka, but here one certainly was, perhaps the very same one I saw in July.

Strangely, walking along the edge of the lake yesterday afternoon to Whakamoenga Point and a possible encounter with a trout, I passed several kaka beak shrubs, all exhibiting those clusters of pinky-red, parrot-beaked flowers that give the plant its name. They had been planted by the Gowers to augment the existing native trees and shrubs which help to make the Whakamoenga Point property such an attractive one.

By the time I had walked in to the edge of Mine Bay the rain had stopped, but the air was still keen, and I was glad indeed of my Barbour jacket and hood. The water looked less promising than it did a few days ago: only a faint northeaster blew, which failed to impress the water surface on the sheltered side. The other day, waves rolled busily around the corner to my left and subsided reluctantly in front of me, no longer driven by the big nor'easter blowing. I may have been right in assuming that, if fish were about, they would be in my vicinity, working round in the "eddy" just around the corner into Mine Bay. Certainly two fish came to the little Red Setter, but they might have come anyway, eddy or no.

Casting and casting the same little Red Setter into the blessedly high and clear water of the lake, I eventually made contact with a fish, and landed her, to the accompaniment of gasps of wonder at her size from an enthusiastic gallery of small children. She was a twin of the second fish I caught the other day: a slimmish rainbow of 1.6kg. When I cleaned her later, I noted that her eggs were at precisely the same stage of development as those of the earlier fish: they were only about one fifth of the size I expected them to be. She was in better condition than the other fish though, and will taste, smoked, almost as good as the jack fish of the other day tasted.

Blooding a new rod

Blackbirds fled before me down the track past the Major Jones Pool. When I had trudged on by they would return, to gobble more of the rich red berries clustered on all the cotoneaster bushes edging the path to Judge's.

Midwinter along the Tongariro can be cold. If you are a trout-fisher you cannot escape the bite of downstream southerly blusters bearing icy reminders of the new deep snows on the mountains. This time, there was even snow on Pihanga and Tihia.

If you are a blackbird, though, you seek the sheltered pathway where the cotoneasters and the pyracanthas offer days and days of red and golden feasting. The ground just there is strewn with berries, but, if Turangi blackbirds are as wasteful as ours in Acacia Bay, the berries on the ground will remain untouched long after the birds have stripped the branches clean.

Walking briskly in thigh boots and hooded jacket, I soon warmed up, but I was later to regret the absence of an extra layer of clothing between jersey and jacket. Standing for a time in Judge's, and then in the head of the Major Jones, my back to the cold gusts, I found myself on the verge of shivering.

Why, anyway, hadn't I put the neoprene waders on? But I knew very well why. I wasn't sure how far I was going to walk that day, and walking any distance in body waders — whether neoprene or not — and then getting into cold river water, predisposes that juxtaposition of temperatures (as the medical profession might say) to saturate the inside of the waders with condensation. Or so I find. But at least neoprene body waders keep the long-range winter fisherman warm, however damp he may be inside them.

However, in tandem with the winter experiment of walking and fishing in thigh boots rather than in clinging body waders, went a theory about long rods rendering deep wading unnecessary. And I carried a long rod — a brand-new, graphite, 6–7 weight, 3.12m rod — which had yet to catch a fish.

The idea was that, because the long rod would achieve far greater casting distance for me than the little 2.6m graphite that has served me so well on lake, river and stream for the past 10 years or so, I would not need to wade very deep at all. Thus I would frighten fewer fish. Thus again, I would need only thigh boots. I was thinking, too, of Whakaipo, where on two recent occasions I had hooked fish surprisingly close to the shore within a very short time of moving heron-like into a cautious start.

I would reach out further with the longer rod and have to wade no deeper to do so.

Until you arrive, all happy and hopeful, at the head of Judge's on the eastern side of the river, you don't know whether or not anyone else is there. My happiness and hopefulness sank into my thigh boots when I found two downstreamers already fishing the pool. Three more anglers were nymphing on the other bank. Distantly downstream, six pygmies opposite the big bluff cast and cast and cast.

Well, gregarious trout-fishing, upstream or down, is not my favourite way of passing a pleasant hour or so, but I stayed and fished for a while. The downstreamer in front of me, waist deep and sporting a brilliant yellow parka, trod his way through what seemed to me to be the most likely holding water on our side of the pool. I wanted to bring reality to my new shallow-wading, long-casting theory, but when a man on the bank is waiting to get in behind you, and the man in front of you remains well within a 20-metre cast of you downstream, and is, moreover, far deeper in the water than your thigh boots will allow you to go — and thus too vulnerable to your size 4 lure at the end of its swing — trying to bring reality to anything but frustration is virtually impossible.

I withdrew, chatted briefly to a new arrival who, like me, ruefully wanted solitude for his fishing, and began the walk back towards the Major Jones.

Blackbirds among the red cotoneaster berries this time fled the other way before me. A brilliant cock yellowhammer jumped up from the track in great surprise at my sudden appearance. Like the colours of the cock goldfinch I was to see later, the colours of the yellowhammer seemed twice as vivid as I remembered them from summertime. But spring, rather than winter, is surely the time when plumage takes on its brightest hues?

Great Scott! The Major Jones Pool was empty! True, my thigh boots would not steer me down the traditional downstreamer's deep route, waist deep, and I wasn't too sure yet of the distance the new rod would cast. And, of course, when you are wading somewhat less than thigh deep in the Major Jones it doesn't matter if you cast 10 metres or 50, your line will still catch on the bottom when it swings directly below you into the much slower and shallower inside water.

Somebody, at some time, had made me a present of twin lures dressed on size 4 hooks. They each sported an overwing of orange marabou above a wasp-yellow body ribbed with black. Well, I stood in the rush of the rapids pelting down into the pool, and cast the first of these colour-mismatched flies upon the waters. I don't fish the Major Jones Pool too often these days, but when I do, and when I have free run of its beginnings, southerly or no southerly, the top 20 metres or so invariably brings a fish to the fly. And so it was again today. Inside 20 minutes I was fast into a fish which jumped and ran, jumped and ran, while I made haste to the shore to get downstream of it.

Once upon an Otamangakau time, when Cliff was there to counsel caution, a fish had battled to and fro, to and fro, for seemingly an age of morning hours. This fish seemed almost as strong, hardly yielding, dourly imposing a will that refused to surrender to a pressure that would bring it into the shallows. Four hours after the Otamangakau fish had come to hand, it weighed a little short of 4.5kg, and so I have always thought of it, there upon the workroom wall, as a 10-pounder. But when the Major Jones fish came sullenly to shore, showing a silver side, I thought at first that it would hardly make half the size of my Otamangakau fish.

I was wrong, as I so often am. According to the spring balance at the motel, that beautiful silver hen rainbow trout weighed exactly 3kg, not far short of 6½lb. I refuse to consider that, in the interests of customer satisfaction, motel management had tampered with the spring balance. Utterly and absolutely I refuse to believe that they would stoop to such despicable tricks. It would be on a level with disconnecting the odometer on a newish car you wanted to sell. Mind you, I once knew a well-respected businessman who used to do just that . . .

So I had blooded the new rod in the head of the Major Jones Pool, and it was a very satisfying thing to have done. I thought I might have achieved an earlier blooding the day before, when, carefully choosing a stretch of water for a first trial of the long rod, I started in at the head of the west bank of Boulder Reach.

That west bank may have shallowed somewhat since the most recent flood, for no fish came my way. Not even a tentative nudge disturbed the afternoon. Perhaps everyone else knew that no fish lay along the reach on my side, for I had the whole place to myself. No matter, the afternoon sun tempered the cold wind, and the dark green sinking line went whistling out to gratifying lengths, and a couple of hours later I went back to three stiff and warming whiskies, thoroughly contented with the performance of a new rod and the vindication of a new shallow-wading theory. Well, part vindication: my thigh boots were wet inside. I thought at first the pair of them were leaking, but no, it was the old problem, condensation, although nowhere near as profound a problem, abetted by fatigue, as is posed by neoprene.

After lunch on Monday I sought the constant winter promise of the other side of Boulder Reach. I would nymph it up, with the floating line, as a further test of the rod. But wind gusted down the reach, and the glare in the south which took its colour from the snow showers sweeping across the snow-capped Kaimanawas, made it hopeless to watch the pale-blue, wind-blown line for telltale movement.

153

It would have been most rewarding to finish the day with a trout taken on a nymph thrown by the new rod. But it wasn't to be. The floating line was a 7-weight, but the rod could not punch it through the wind. Should I step up to an 8-weight? Surely not; the shorter graphite is itself an 8-weight, thereby demanding a 9-weight line for optimum performance. But I have never been able to handle any line heavier than a 7-weight on it. By the same token, in theory, the new long rod, and I, would be happiest with a 6-weight line, perhaps even a 5-weight, even though, when down-streaming duty calls, the old Hardy 7-weight level line will again respond sweetly, slipping smoothly through the rings to great distances. After all, the rod is rated 6–7, so I shall buy a 6-weight line, a slow sinker, say, and take careful note of the effort (preferably lack of effort) necessary to deliver 25 metres of it, time after time, to its destination.

I shall experiment, too, with the 5-weight floater that I normally reserve for the Waipunga. Someone said the length of the new rod would help to overcome the riverside toetoe problem along the Waipunga, and I am sure that it will; but while long rods do have certain advantages over short ones, disadvantages invest them too, notably when it comes to line, tippet or fly mix-ups at the top of the rod.

Short rods are user-friendly on those occasions. They quickly allow you, waist deep perhaps, to unravel line from a top joint, or feed a lure back through the top ring, say, without having to go ashore to do so. Provided the problem can be solved with one hand, it's no trouble to hold the rod roughly halfway along in the other hand: the top ring can readily be reached.

But I couldn't do that with the long rod. It doesn't seem a point of great significance, and perhaps my impatience is rarely shared by others, but when the fly, for some reason, wraps tightly round the top few centimetres of the rod, or lodges in the top ring, or, worse still, pops through the top ring and hangs down between that one and the next, the short rod is a blessing and the long one is a curse. The short one saves you time, whereas the long one demands that you go ashore.

However, putting aside the going-ashore nuisance, and possibly the drawback of a rod that weighs heavier in the hand, the advantages are considerable: longer casts achieved with less energy; slower, more deliberate timing; the likelihood of fewer frightened fish; and the background obstacles that can now be cleared on the back-cast.

My Turangi stay was all too brief. I would have liked to explore more of the river, noting where the recent flood had reshaped banks and pools. I could have done some of that kind of exploring the next morning, before heading back to Taupo, but I found the eastern side of Judge's empty of anglers, and these days when the Tongariro advertises a vacancy, you must book in straightaway.

I hope I don't sound too smug, too I-told-you-so, but just where the man in the yellow parka had stood the day before, I hooked a strong jack rainbow on a pale Red Setter. He was a most unwilling captive. He jumped and ran and bored down deep, and jumped and ran again. I thought he might weigh the same as yesterday's hen. In fact he was half a kilo lighter, but no less fit; yet another worthy example of this year's run of big Tongariro rainbows.

Gillett's Bay

For those who don't know, Gillett's Bay lies about a 10-minute shoreline walk past Willow Point, which itself marks the southern extremity of the little bay at Whakaipo lying to the left of the Mapara Stream's entry into Lake Taupo.

Halfway to Gillett's today, I came across the remains of what was most likely the vanquished drake of the three paradise ducks — two drakes and a duck — that had crossed the stage of a recent Saturday morning's fishing. The gorgeously plumaged bird lay quite dead on the beach, surrounded by a litter of fine soft feathers. Virtually bare, and showing ugly red marks, the drake's neck had been the target of either another drake or a black swan. The bird had been throttled to death, I would say, and not so long before, because it was still quite whole. Pigs and feral cats live on that shore and yet the dead bird had not been touched.

I would touch it, though, on the way back from my fishing at Gillett's. Soft rust-reds, deeper and striated rust-reds, speckled black-and-whites, and near-blacks from wing-primaries, promised a treasure-trove of rare feathers for fly-tying.

Meanwhile, Gillett's Bay beckoned. If the wind blows from the south, pushing waves onto the beach to the left of the stream, you need walk no further than the couple of hundred metres to Willow Point and fish slowly back towards the stream-mouth. But if the wind blows from the north, I find it better to go with it as far as Gillett's. The idea there is to wade out at the northern end, keeping in the lee of the big rocks, and throw a fly

155

across the wind, so that it comes back on the retrieve in the deepish water at the head of the bay.

Mind you, if you can't throw a fly at right angles to a wind coming from your right, you can forget about Gillett's — or anywhere else requiring consistent safe casting in the same direction. What you have to do is either cast hastily over the right shoulder (if you're right-handed) and hope that the sunglasses you're wearing will stop an errant hook, or cast over your left shoulder. The latter option is the better one, although I am told that repeated casting over the left shoulder will bring on tennis elbow in right-handed casters. And that's probably true; it seems no time at all since tennis elbow in my right arm almost put paid to my fishing for some weeks. The odd thing was, though, that while I had undoubtedly been a frequent over-the-left-shoulder caster for some weeks leading up to the affliction, my left arm also became affected, and I don't cast left-handed.

I risked tennis elbow this morning for the hour of casting I gave myself at Gillett's. The wind blew strongly at times over my right shoulder, building waves which grew and died as the wind itself grew and died. No trout

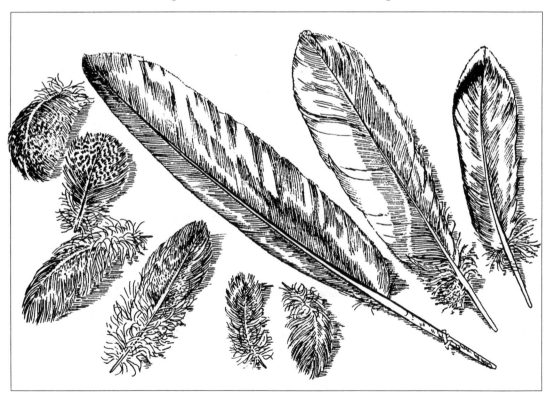

broached, and no smelt or bully appeared in the heaving waters around me.

Half an hour after I had started, however, a fish came at the small green Hairy Dog. I felt it twice in the space of a second, but nothing was there when I tried to make contact.

Away to the south, walls of rain swept across the lake. The singing birds of an hour before — thrushes, grey warblers, whiteheads, a bellbird and a chaffinch — stayed silent. Cloud straggled damply across the sky, and then I was suddenly aware of an ominous dark-grey mass looming up over the shadowed hills opposite. And was that a distant rumble of thunder?

I didn't quite make it back to the car before the rain came pelting in from the northwest, blotting out the view across the bay. Fortunately the squall quickly spent itself, and finished up with a flash of lightning and a deafening drum roll of thunder just as I opened the boot of the car. I dismantled my lethal carbon-fibre lightning conductor and stowed it away in record time.

Hysteria at Whakaipo

After an hour of casting and retrieving the green-bodied Hairy Dog at Whakaipo, I became thoroughly resigned to yet another Lake Taupo blank. No trout broached. Not even a single bully or smelt that I could see swam among the rocks and the short lacy filaments of green weed around me.

True, it would be a two-hour blank at most. It wasn't as if I had stumbled out of the house bleary-eyed in the wee small hours to tackle a legal marathon of 19 hours of fishing. No way. I had swallowed a mug of tea at 10 o'clock of a fine Sunday morning and left Margaret to cope with small granddaughter Jessica, whom she loves dearly. It wasn't altogether a self-indulgent act on my part to go fishing. The grass had been cut not too many days before. I had worked industriously in the garden. And it was well known on all sides that I was long overdue for a more generous amount of fishing time — especially because, since I had been semi-retired for two months, my workload had in fact substantially increased.

Hysteria greeted my arrival at Whakaipo. A paradise duck shrieked her disapproval of life in general, and me in particular, as though it and I more nearly resembled hell than paradise. She carried on her frenzied calls for the five minutes it took me to walk around the shore to the big

157

pine tree, and then she put in 10 more minutes of her mad and maddening screams. She was surely Shakespeare's original shrew, and I can't say I envied either of the two drakes who happened to be accompanying her at the time. One of them took off and flew strongly south when I appeared down the track leading to the mouth of the Mapara Stream. I can't say I blamed him for using me as an excuse to fly well out of range of that infuriating sound. The other male (a bird who has much to learn about women) stayed chivalrously alongside the complainant, solacing her with the there-there sounds typical of shelduck drakes when their women scream, and scream, and scream. Fancy putting up with that noise for the lifetime that these birds spend together.

Behind me, the mountains of the Tongariro National Park thrust snow-covered slopes and peaks into a clear blue sky. The steady breeze came straight off them, and though the sun shone bravely, I was very glad indeed of my quilted green jacket and neoprene body waders. Some people try to tell us that the first of September is the first day of spring, but this morning's temperature made it quite plain that spring was yet some way off. Even though the steady chill breeze of morning spent itself shortly after midday, enough of winter remained throughout my two hours at Whakaipo for me to be grateful for the warmth of the clothing I wore. But at least the chill breeze blew steadily, one way, all the time I was there. So often, changeable breezes throw the fish off balance. As long as a ripple, or even a mild attacking surf, preserves an unchanging course, trout seem readier to respond, however cold the day.

Mind you, an aura of spring prevailed. The beginnings of the slender leaves of summer misted all the willows along the shore. Mallard swam about in pairs. Tiny plants thrust through the stones and flotsam on the shore.

And what a shore it was! After the virtual drought of winter, which covered the shrunken northeastern beaches with a mess of stinking weed piled high, the bay lay wonderfully clean and bright under the morning sunshine. Close to the mouth of the stream the lake lapped refreshingly clean sandy beaches.

As usual, I was enjoying the accompaniments of fly-fishing without fish: the snowy mountains way down south; the evidence that spring was at hand; the calling of whiteheads; the ringing monotony of a kingfisher and his sudden swift flight past me; the disapproving withdrawal of a heron; the distant cries of lambs from the Whakaipo paddocks.

But it's rewarding to catch a fish, too; so when the hesitant take came, at long last, and when I had driven the hook home, I enjoyed coaxing a

strong hen rainbow ashore. She would have weighed no more than a kilo-gram, and yet she jumped and jumped, and would not easily surrender. I freed her quickly and sent her back into the lake.

Not long afterwards, the Hairy Dog had only just started to sink at the end of yet another cast when a trout took hold. I was still waiting for the fly to reach an acceptable level when the line pulled tight. Flustered, I clumsily returned the pull. Fish are not meant to upset time-honoured routines. For instance, they are meant to wait until the lure sinks to a proper depth and begins to move jerkily through the water before engulf-ing it, aren't they? This one didn't know the rules.

The next moment I knew I was attached to the heaviest fish I had ever encountered at Whakaipo. All the fly-line went in a rush, followed by most of the backing. Quite suddenly the screech of the reel stopped, but line continued to stream out. Backing was freewheeling on the spool. Would I ever land the monster?

Earlier, the hysterical paradise duck, screaming threats, had taken off in pursuit of a drake which had flown over. Now, in the middle of my dan-gerously attenuated connection with a large fish, three paradise ducks came flighting in to my end of the bay. Luckily they flew well above the height of the backing stretching away into the distance. But even if they had flown lower they wouldn't have seen the line: two of the three were oblivious of everything except the third bird. When I had first arrived at the bay, two drakes and a hysterical duck had made their presence exces-sively apparent. I was now faced with a single drake and two shrieking ducks. Didn't they carry on, those termagants! Anyone would have thought that the object of the ducks' attention just happened to be the very last paradise duck drake left alive in the whole wide world.

In the meantime, my fish allowed me to recover 20 metres of line be-fore stripping off another 30 metres. I guessed it was a rainbow of about 4kg. After a long time the backing came tightly back on the reel, and then most of the fly-line. Finally the fish — and the truth — surfaced. It wasn't such a big fish at all. In fact it weighed a little under 2kg on the kitchen scales at home — and that included the four hefty bullies in its stomach.

For its length it ought to have weighed more, but you do occasionally come across a lake fish which will rush away unstoppably for 60 or 70 metres. When you lose these customers, your anguish compels them to weigh at least 4kg, maybe 5kg.

What a comedown when you land them!

160